CURIOUS WILTSHIRE

Cover: Cherhill White Horse

Road to Curious Wiltshire

CURIOUS WILTSHIRE

Mary Delorme

With photographs by Duncan Skene

EX LIBRIS PRESS

First published 1985

Reprinted with corrections 1987

Ex Libris Press
1 The Shambles
Bradford on Avon
Wiltshire

Cover by 46 Design, Bradford on Avon

Typeset in 11 on 13 point Baskerville
by Saxon Printing Ltd., Derby
Printed by A.Wheaton and Co., Exeter

ISBN 0 948578 00 9

Acknowledgements

My thanks are primarily due to Roger Jones, one of the two most patient publishers in the business, and to Dr.John Chandler, Local Studies Officer of Wiltshire Library and Museum Service, whose unique knowledge of Wiltshire is always so graciously shared.

I must also thank the staffs of Devizes Museum, Wiltshire Record Office, and Trowbridge Library for their assistance. The Church Commissioners and the Ministry of Agriculture instructed me upon latter-day tithes and the internal arrangements of sheep, and Mr George Bradbury kindly compared notes on Blind Houses. I am especially grateful to farmers and clergy who spared time to answer a stranger's questions, and to Miss Burnett-Brown of the National Trust.

Primus inter pares is the determinedly anonymous gentleman who coined the immortal phrase – "Leave the washing-up."

Dedication

For Phyl and Laurie Bowring who directed my footsteps towards Bradford on Avon.

CONTENTS

About the author: Mary Delorme has been a writer for many years, and moved to Trowbridge twenty years ago. At first her published work consisted mainly of music, but since coming to Wiltshire she has had over seventy articles published, largely on education, history, topography and biography, for journals such as *History Today, The Teacher* and *The Historian*. For five years she was a regular reviewer for *Primary Education Review*. Her books include one educational title, *Doctors*, which was recommended by the B.B.C. for use in conjunction with schools T.V. A novel about modern musicians, *Wandering Minstrels*, was published last year; an historical novel, *Alexis*, on the life of the great chef Soyer, is complete, and to be published in February 1986. At present she is writing a book on *Curiosities of the Sussex Countryside*, after which there are several commissions to fulfil.

Her son, Jon, is a professional photographer who frequently illustrates her work, but at the time of writing his own has taken him to California.

INTRODUCTION

The book neared completion, and my publisher suggested an introduction explaining why Wiltshire had aroused my curiosity.

Our Surrey beauty spot was too full of film crews and their paper cups; Bath was a tempting alternative, though house hunting meant travelling across a wide open space called Wiltshire. Everything has its price.

After the Surrey house had been sold, the Bath purchase fell through, but there was a cottage in Trowbridge. We went, muttering. We stayed.

It was a spacious house built in the time of Jane Austen, with a rose walk in which she might appear at any moment. Upstairs there were views across a wide valley of farmland to a hillside on which a great white horse had been cut in the chalk.

Back in the shabby town, we parked on cobble-stones and gazed. The Parade, that grand row of cloth merchants' mansions, had just been cleaned; pale, immaculate and beautiful. We strolled down to the river, and found a small stone house. A house – without windows? There was a plaque on the side; it was my first Blind House.

That was twenty years ago; twenty years in which to explore hill forts like Bratton Castle, realising the need of the earlier inhabitants for a vast, clear view to forestall attack; to have primitive dewponds for themselves and their livestock in case of seige. I felt for medieval farmers; however meagre their crops, tithes must still be taken to those dim barns; was it desperation which turned their descendants to the development of water meadows, or just the sturdy common sense by which they utilised so much of the sarsen stone lying at their feet?

Twenty years .... too brief a time in which to satisfy my curiosity about this wide open space called Wiltshire; but come with me ....

Mary Delorme
Trowbridge
Wiltshire
July 1985

DRAMATIS PERSONAE

Aitken, John, 1839-1919: son of a Falkirk lawyer. Briefly studied engineering, but his health failed and he spent his declining years (approximately sixty of them) in experimental physics. His best-known conclusion is that "condensation in air saturated with water vapour is brought about by the vapour's condensing on individual dust particles of the other nuclei in the air". This fact was used by C.T.R.Wilson in making the Wilson Cloud Chamber. Elected F.R.S. 1889.

Aubrey, John (1625-1697): In later years Aubrey recalled that a body of students – Yorke, Gore, Daniel, Sir Joseph Ernely, Nicholas (afterwards Judge) and self, met in 1659 proposing to write a history of Wiltshire by division ("parcel it out between them") but the design vanished "in fumo tabaci". Not by any means; we still treasure his *Natural History of Wiltshire.*

Blyth, Edward (1810-1873): No advantages; self-taught. Studied in the small hours and his articles of natural history were published and highly esteemed before he was twenty. Went to India as zoologist and became one of the foremost of his time, though never any material rewards. One of his youthful articles was the one on dew.

Leland, John (c.1506-1552): King's Antiquary appointed to Henry VIII; the first and only such appointment. Leland travelled country-wide, examining ancient monuments, particularly the archives, of priories, abbeys, cathedrals, etc., in the hope of preventing the destruction of valuable MSS.

Martin, Edward (1865-1943): Elected Fellow Royal Geological Society 1895, awarded a three-year fellowship to study dew ponds; published: *Dew Ponds; History, Observation and Experiment* (Werner Laurie 1914).

Plenderleath, Revd. William Charles, Vicar of Cherhill 1860-91, died 1906. A leading member of the Wiltshire Archaeological Society, sometime its secretary. Wrote numerous papers of value, and had a sense of humour.

Wells, William Charles (1757-1817): Born South Carolina of Scottish immigrants. Studied at St.Bartholomew's Hospital under William Hunter; returned to Florida and ran a newspaper. Back in England, was Physician to St.Thomas' Hospital. Publications included *Essay on Dew* (1814).

THE MAPS accompanying the text show the main sites of the features of Wiltshire which are discussed. They are not meant to be exhaustive lists; sites have been chosen bearing in mind interest and accessibility.

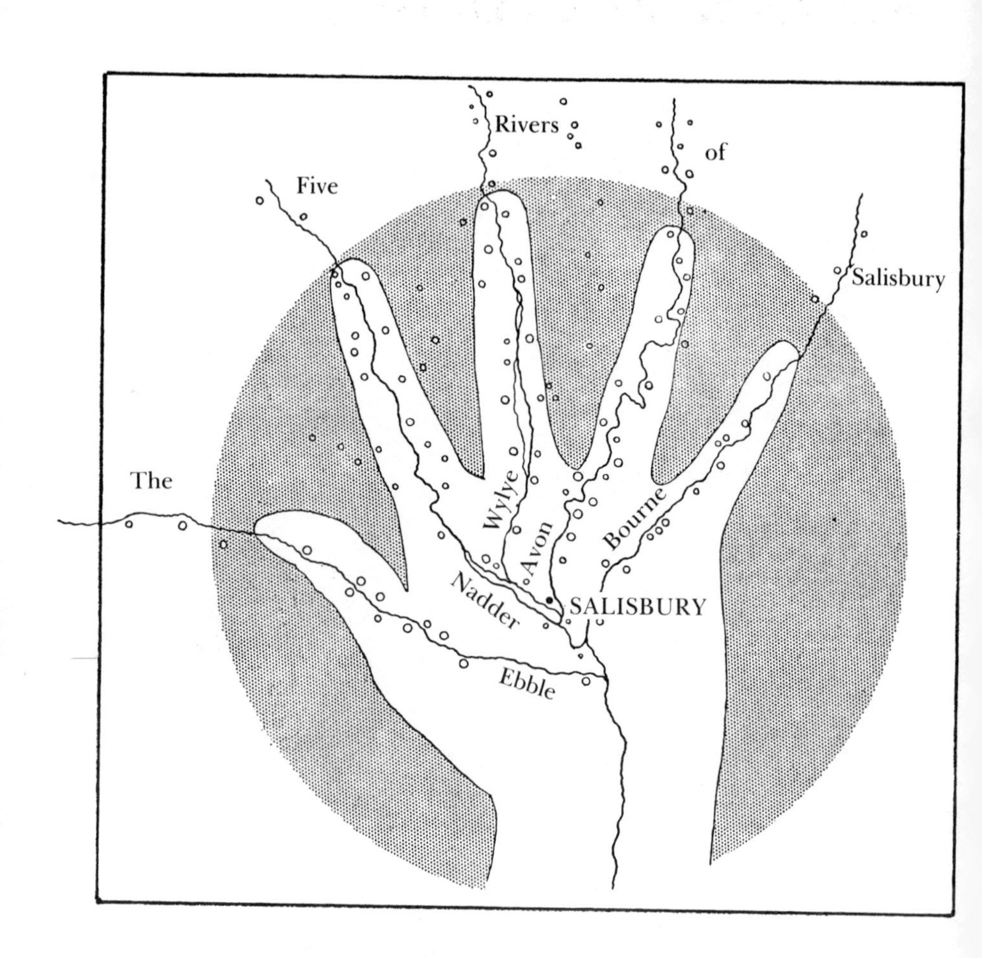

WATER MEADOWS The five rivers of South Wiltshire; although they can be found near most of Wiltshire's rivers, South Wiltshire was the nearest thing to perfection for water meadows, with its light soil over fine flint and gravel with clear-running streams of warm water. The River Kennet in north-east Wiltshire also once fed an intricate system of water meadows. (Figure after W.H.Hudson: *A Shepherd's Life,* 1910; page 9)

WATER MEADOWS

Wiltshire shepherds were not the Arcadian beings of poetic imagery, neither were they the keen-eyed hunters of Biblical lore. They were men of patience and endurance, with expertise which was usually the accumulated experience of generations – a treasury of wisdom which few presumed to question. They were, in effect, the rulers of the downland pastures. Normally one shepherd was in charge, not of one flock, but the flocks of an entire community; a very important person.

He had a strangely named counterpart: the drowner, who worked mainly in the broad valleys between the downlands, harnessing water from the chalk rivers for a highly specialised form of irrigation. Water meadows were for centuries a dominant feature of Wiltshire agriculture. Long straight drains, cutting across the meadows, were at first sight akin to the rhines of the Somerset wetlands; but whereas the latter were intended to drain water off the land, water meadows were primarily to bring it on, in an ingeniously controlled flow. Great grain crops were harvested in the southern area of the county, and Wiltshire sheep were kept mainly as a necessary aid to their production. The dung was an ideal fertiliser, and the hooves, carrying a suitable body weight, were perfect instruments for compacting the earth to the right consistency for sowing.

There was one great difficulty. March and April were barren months for people with sheep to feed. Winter hay was either sparse or spent; spring pasture was not yet ready. Yet the ewes were lambing, and adequate food was essential. The sole possibility was young wheat and clover, destined for the later hay crop. Ewes with spring lambs had to eat that, and later in the year hay must be purchased elsewhere, with the additional cost of transport.

It was a problem to which water meadows provided a solution in Wiltshire and other counties, though their beginnings were largely unrecorded and long forgotten. In 1850, the Royal Agricultural Society chose Exeter as the venue for their annual week-long gathering, and water meadows figured prominently among the attractions. On the morning of Friday July 19th, Mr Turner of Barton conducted members around his water meadows; the same afternoon they were similarly received by Sir Thomas Acland at Killerton. On the following Monday, they visited those of the Duke of Portland at Clipstone Park: "In coming to Devonshire (members) will have an opportunity of witnessing that celebrated system of irrigation which has been successfully practised from the remotest times, which though attended with some expense, is one of the most profitable improvements .... the pride of Devonshire agriculture before which the celebrity of its cream, cattle and cider must give way."

From the remotest times: no one could recall the beginnings, no one claimed credit for the invention. Early in 1799, T.Wright published *The Art of Floating Land*, as practised in the County of Gloucester. Obviously the art was well established there. But the only account of any inception of the idea was written in Herefordshire, by a man who worked out the system by trial and error in the latter years of Elizabeth Tudor.

In the Beginning

Rowland Vaughan was a very young kinsman of Blanche Parry; that formidable woman who was for so many years the dear friend of the Queen. Great-aunt Blanche had already sponsored Rowland's cousin at Court – he had risen to be Groom of the Chambers. Great things were expected of the newcomer.

He was no milksop – just a youngster needing time and experience before he could cope with domineering people. Whether he was gauche or merely shy, he failed to please

Blanche. In later years he wrote of her "crabbed austerity" and "the bitterness of her humour;" she nagged him for a few years, then lost patience and sent him off to the Irish wars. Food, if any, was bad; the weather was worse, and the countryside so bleak that he was often waist-deep in bogs. He served for three years before being invalided out, and returned to Herefordshire, where his family had a minor stately home near the River Wye.

Apart from the hunting, Rowland was bored; he was about to set off for the Lowland wars when he met pretty cousin Elizabeth Parry, and for the first time in his life he found that he was pleasing everyone, himself included. She was enchanting and affectionate – and wealthy. Her manor was in the Golden Valley to the west of Hereford, near his own home. All the Vaughans and Parrys were delighted; they had been numerous enough for generations of intermarriage, and Elizabeth's fortune was yet another to be kept safely in the family.

After the wedding, Rowland found that something else had been kept in the family. Though not yet Blanche's equal, his bride had inherited that lady's talent for verbal warfare, and the best place for a peaceable warrior was out of doors, though even there freedom was unattainable. Various cronies with whom he had shared the Irish experiences, and whose fellowship had cheered his convalescence, were now forbidden. Such low company was unsuitable for Elizabeth's husband; contrariwise, it was quite suitable for him to visit her mill and put the miller in his place – a rogue like the rest of his kind, and sure to defraud her unless supervised. Rowland's pleas that a servant could do it as well or better went unheeded.

He stood moodily in the chill of a March day, watching the stream as it approached the mill, and trying to summon enough resolution to follow it and see the miller.

Instead, he saw a molehill; an unusually large one on the bank, like a hillock. The mole had tunnelled so close to the waterline that a little stream of water – a "waterprill" - turned away from the main channel, through the molehill, and down the gently sloping field; it spread thinly, about one pace wide and twenty paces long. The winter had been dry, and the ground was parched, but wherever the waterprill trickled, everything was green and fresh.

In that moment, Rowland's mind was aflame with new purpose.

By accident the mole had made parched, compacted earth come to life in the least fertile season. Born a countryman, and now a landowner, Rowland was familiar with agricultural problems. This was a grand solution to one of the worst, and it must be done on a grand scale. It would need co-operation from his neighbours and tenants; he would need tact, firmness, guile, every possible means of persuasion; his timidity had gone forever.

His little book, *Water-Workes*, was not written until about twenty years after his inspiration; he took about six years to write it, and it was published in 1610. It is significant that in recounting events before the birth of the idea, he described everything as belonging to others - "Her Father's house;" "Her miller;" "Her manor;" his or hers – never Rowland's. Yet after the inspiration his language changed. "My mill;" "My tenant;" "My ground;" – he had assumed command. Even though he was writing so long after the initial events, emotion remained fresh in his mind. From that time, he was truly lord of his manor. Whatever he designed, whatever he planned – all orders must be obeyed.

Friends and Neighbours

It was complicated. Meadows must be disciplined into an intricate system of trenches, ridges and drains, conducting water from the river and converting it into a shallow, continuously moving film which would protect and nourish without swamping. The trenches and drains must be lined, preferably with wood, so that the sides would not collapse under the weight of water. The gradient of the land was important; there must be enough force behind the flow to ensure sufficient movement to avoid stagnation.

Friends and neighbours; some declared that Rowland was out of his wits; others, won over by his new confidence, joined with him in land and effort. Eventually there were many miles of water meadows in operation. After two or three years' trial and error many scoffers were converted; the scheme was working.

Even in the Golden Valley, farmers had shared the same old problem with everyone else. Winter hay had gone by March, or April at the latest; ewes and spring lambs needed food. Now, they could be sure of the best. "My Drownings" as Rowland called them, could be controlled at will. When necessary, the river could be diverted along his system of carriers and drains, lightly covering the meadows, protecting the roots of the grass from winter cold, encouraging growth where before there had been discouragement. When the ground was wet enough, there were sluices to turn the river back to its normal course; there were turves, cut to size, ready to stop the flow along smaller channels. Regularly, from autumn and through the winter, the meadows were drowned, then dried. When some growth appeared, they were drowned again. Then, in March, the water was shut off for at least three weeks before the ewes and lambs came to feed on the tender new grass. When their normal pasture was ready, they went to it; the water meadows were drowned yet again, then left to produce an extra hay crop.

Naturally there were setbacks and disappointments through the years. Friends were not infallibly friendly under Rowland's demanding regime; not every neighbour was anxious to add his land to the scheme, though the water flow was easier to regulate over a larger area. However, news travelled. Rowland had been at work for about five years when Blanche, aged and blind but alert to the last, left evidence of belated approval in her will. Remembering their former relationship, the number of other Vaughans and Parrys with expectations, and the value of money at that period, a legacy of £100 was indeed liberal. News of Rowland's water meadows travelled further than the Court; visitors made long journeys to see the work. One gentleman told him that it was "of late, a common thing in Devonshire, but not in so ample a manner."

Not only in Devon; also in Dorset and Wiltshire. There were experienced "drowners" recorded as working in those counties early in the seventeenth century; Rowland began his project early in the 1580s. There appear to be no definite records of sixteenth century water meadows in the West Country, except that, according to Rowland's visitors, they were well established at the same time as his own, and therefore the idea was not derived from his work. Bearing in mind the position of those counties - every one bordering on Somerset – it seems possible that the originators may have been inspired by work in the Somerset wetlands.

Water Meadow Country: River Wylye and its flood plain at Norton Bavant

Water in the West Country

That county, so close a neighbour, had from time immemorial been plagued by a water surplus; much of the land was below sea level, easily overwhelmed by tides rushing inland for almost twenty miles, the floodwater controlled only by a complicated system of rhines and drains needing unremitting care. Drainage had been a cause for concern, and floods a source of terror, for centuries. Parish records contain many like this item entered in mid-eighteenth century by the churchwarden of Whaddon in Wiltshire: "Gafe 8 famileayes that the sea Dround out"(amount unspecified) .

Some fifteenth century taxes were levied specifically for drainage purposes, and not only for Somerset. Henry VIII was frequently concerned about coastal erosion in Kent and "Southsex" and commissioners appointed by the Court of Sewers (1532) were well occupied in the marshes of Pevensey and Romney, and in the maintenance of sluice gates in various tidal rivers. Water was an ancient problem; whether it had to be persuaded onto the land, or drained off, ingenuity was necessary and mistakes were costly.

In Somerset effort was directed towards its removal. Some observant owner of parched pasture may have wondered: if ditches, drains and sluices can control such powerful forces, even when emanating from the sea, surely rivers and springs might similarly be harnessed and made to flow where and when they were needed?

One of the great agricultural authorities of the late eighteenth century was Thomas Davis; agent to the Marquess of Bath, a nobleman much occupied by affairs of state, whose Wiltshire estates were left in Davis' capable hands. So capable indeed, that when the then Board of Agriculture decided to obtain an account of the state of agriculture in every county, the man chosen to write about Wiltshire was Davis. The resultant book included a lengthy section upon water meadows: "The idea of taking the water off the land at will and bringing it on again at will, is the effect of art; and the knowledge of the proper time to do this, the effect of observation."

The Drowner

Observation by many generations had emphasised the cardinal rule; however evenly the water was distributed, however efficiently it was returned to its parent river, nothing could be left to chance; there were times when immediate drainage was vital, more important even than irrigation. The ancient slogan of all drowners – "You lets the water on at the trot and off at the gallop" – was true in more ways than one. On at the trot to banish the bogey of those early barren months; but always be watchful and ready to drain off at the gallop, for even the briefest overdrowning would cause stagnation, damaging those precious roots. Fortunately over-drowning could be seen by the naked eye; a faint trace of scum on the surface would send the drowner and his men quickly to work.

In spite of the mundane title, the Wiltshire drowner was a leader of men. Rowland Vaughan, feeling his way between inspiration and inexperience, was his own drowner, with a similar authority self-imposed. His first and best workman had been very capable, but as soon as success became apparent he demanded some of the credit for the idea. "There grew up a brabble between us" – and he disappeared from the story. Henceforth, whenever Rowland had to go away from home, the meadows always deteriorated.

Matters were different in Wiltshire. The drowner was not lord of the manor, but he was a highly respected craftsman. He was paid by the community to operate all the local watermeadows; there was a considerable area under his authority, for only in that way would maximum efficiency be maintained. Whether his skills were passed from father to son, or from master to pupil, the drowner was an expert and a personage; everyone, with the possible exception of the squire and the parson, deferred to his judgement - even the most authoritarian miller. Occasionally the local water supply had to be shared between them. A typical arrangement would be for the drowner to divert river water to his meadows from Saturday sunset until dawn on Monday; the river would be left in its normal course for the miller's use on Monday, Tuesday and Wednesday; the final three days were allocated according to need, but the drowner's word was final. Considering that Rowland Vaughan, in his early days as lord of the manor, was reluctant to bandy words with his miller, it appears that the drowner was indeed a person to be reckoned with.

His knowledge of the land was necessarily comprehensive; the soil, the subsoil and whatever lay beneath; the contours of the land, the slightest deviation from level, and the location of each deviation; the river water, its origins, and the different places through which it passed. He must know thoroughly the owners and tenants who employed him; however much he may be king of the castle, a wise man would realise that there were better ways of imposing his will than "get down, you dirty rascal." He depended upon willing and able helpers; many a drowner must have learned, like Rowland, the difficulties of working without them. Even when the water meadows were well established, constant care was necessary; when they were being installed, or "floated", massive effort was essential.

River Wylye with water crowfoot at Longbridge Deverill

Different Types of Water Meadow

There were two types: the catchwork, and the floating meadow, the former being simpler, both in floating and maintenance. It was used on hillsides, and the probability was that this was what Rowland's visitor had seen in Devon; Mr Turner, of Barton, had taken the Royal Agricultural Society on a tour of his catchment meadows that Friday morning in 1850. Standing in awe before Rowland's array of trenches-royall, topping trenches, braving and traversing trenches and bastard sluices, all flowing in Golden Valley, the visitor recalled the simple catchment systems of Devon as "not so ample."

A stream running down a hillside was taken as a ready-made main carrier, while a new carrier was cut at right angles, across the hillside as far as necessary, and stopped (temporarily sealed) at both ends. A sluice at the stream end released the water to flow along the new carriage; on reaching the stop at the other end, water would overflow down the hillside.

"The water would soon cease to run equally for any great length, and would wash the land out in gutters." So said Thomas Davis; the problem was solved by catching the water in parallel trenches, every twenty or thirty feet, each one filling and giving a new, even overflow to the next section of the hillside. Those trenches had to be carefully lined with wood, or their lower edges could be washed away within days. Even after an overflow, some water remained in the parallel trenches; it was run off by a deep drain at right angles to them, down to the main drain along the foot of the incline. That main drain might be used to water ground at a lower level, or the water could be returned to the original stream.

Davis estimated that to float such a meadow would cost perhaps £3-£5 per acre, and certainly no more than seven shillings and sixpence per acre for upkeep.

Concerning flowing meadows, Davis, from the depth of his experience, said that they were often started on nothing more promising than a flat morass. Getting the water on and off was achieved only by much heavy labour, and the difficulty of the task was directly affected by the subsoil. In North Wiltshire it was clay; indifferent stuff for water meadows, but excellent for dairy herds; that district was known as cheese country.

South Wiltshire was the nearest thing to perfection for drowners; light soil over fine flint and gravel with clear-running chalk streams of warm water - rarely below forty-five degrees; perfect protection for tender shoots. That being so, the labour was worth while, and the process developed through the centuries.

A ditch, or carrier, was cut all along the higher edge of the meadow at right angles to the river. Then it made another right-angled turn, to go the full length of the meadow as a side carrier.

The ground was dug and piled into a series of long banks, lying parallel with the main carrier at the higher end. Along the top of each bank a channel, or drawn, was cut, along which water flowed from the side carrier. From the drawns smaller finger-like channels sloped away alternately from one side and then the other, distributing water as evenly as possible all over the banks. The end of each drawn was stopped, forcing the water down the sides of the banks rather than leaving the surplus to run off the far end. It ran into the valleys between the beds, where ditches (drains) took it back in the direction of the river. Along the end of the banks a large "tail drain", parallel to the river, received the contents of the other drains. As it reached the end of the meadow, the tail drain curved slightly towards the river bank so that all the water returned from whence it came. The far ends of the drains were also stopped to force the flow back towards the tail drain and the river.

Though this was the basic plan, there were many variations according to the individual characteristics of different meadows. The entire system was adaptable. Perhaps the most sagacious part of the whole enterprise was its organisation under one full-time expert as a single venture, rather than the usual score of smaller owners each struggling to be his own expert. Indeed, the tenants of Henry Hastings struck an intriguingly modern note in 1629; they demanded "A Great Debate" – in order to arrange for the watering of their meadows. They would have met little opposition, for it was generally accepted that properly run water meadows considerably increased the value of the land – even though the cost of floating this type of meadow could be anything

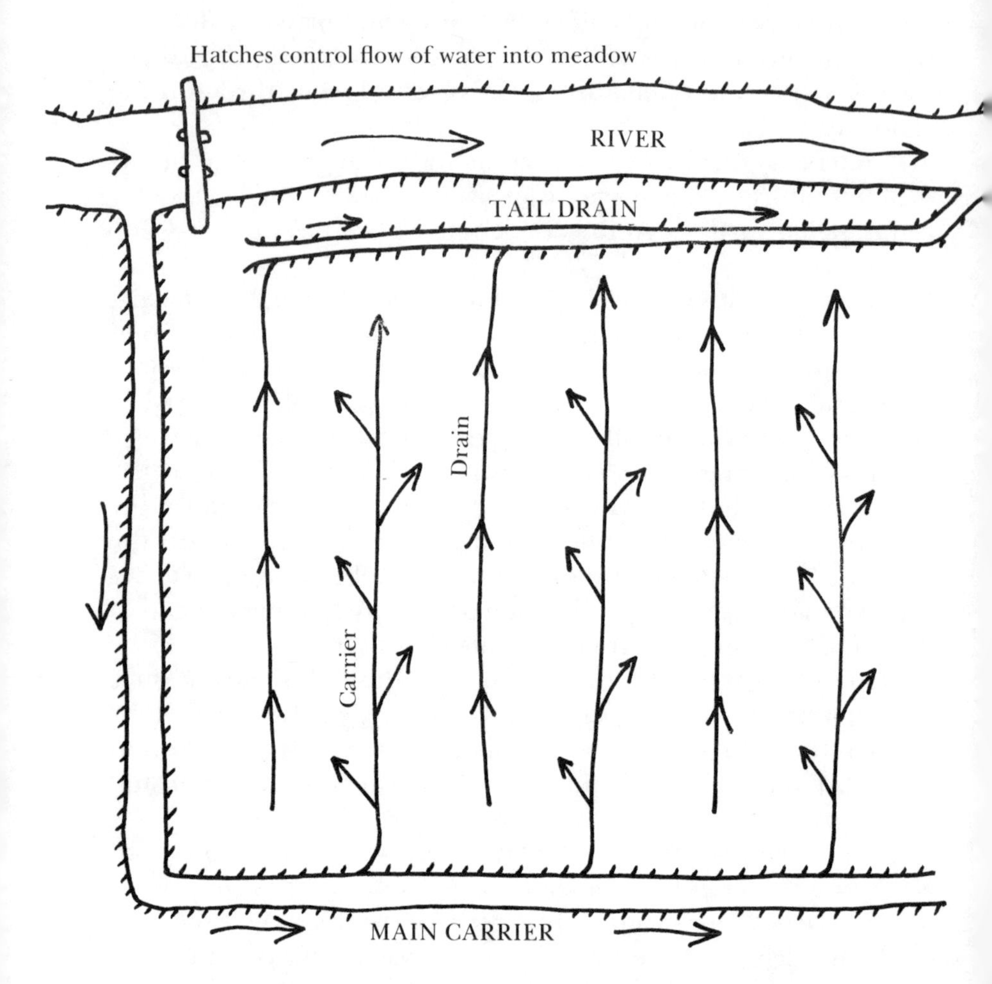

Diagram showing the operation of a Water Meadow (after A Guide to Industrial Archaeology in Wiltshire, 1978)

from twelve to twenty pounds per acre. This enormous variation depended upon the state of the land, and therefore the cost of labour, and the type of hatchwork installed. Hatches, or sluices, must be very strong and made to measure in order to control the fast-flowing chalk streams. They might be made of wood, variable in price and quality, or iron. Somehow there grew a tradition that at some time there had been a vogue for the use of hatches made in Holland; Dutch hatches. While the idea of water control automatically brings the Dutch to mind, there is also a possibilty that those hatches labelled "Dutch" were made by Mr Dutch, an iron founder of Warminster.

The description of the floating of a water meadow may sound complicated, but not too onerous a task, until one takes into account some typical measurements.

Each bed, two hundred yards long and thirty to forty feet wide; each bed from eighteen to twenty-four inches high, and the drawn – the channel along the top – could be twenty inches wide at its junction with the carrier, tapering to only twelve inches at the end. This tapering was necessary to regulate the flow. Conversely, the drains between the beds started at only about eight inches wide, expanding to two feet at the junction with the main drain. The contents of the drains increased as the main drawn and its little upper tributaries sent their contents down the sides of the beds; hence the usually accepted meaning of "on at the trot" - via the large hatch controlling the river flow into the main carrier; and "off at the gallop" – the gradually increasing flow from the drawns along the crown of each great bed, into all the widening drains, and finally from the great tail drain back to the river. In works of such size, the force of the water was indeed powerful. The meadows were an achievement superbly conceived and accomplished, and the farmers felt well repaid by the results.

The chalk country had for centuries produced heavy crops of grain for which well-manured soil was essential. Not only was the best manure for the purpose that of sheep, but Wiltshire had its own breed, the Wiltshire Horn. As meat, it was unremarkable. The wool was good, though not plentiful; it was used in the manufacture of broadcloth which sold at home and abroad at a high price – between twelve and sixteen shillings a yard. There were many busy villages where most of the population were cloth

Hatches to control the flow at Lower Woodford in the valley of the Salisbury Avon

Hatches or sluices of concrete and iron to control the flow at Avon Bridge on the Salisbury Avon

makers working in their own homes. The cloth makers needed bread, and for bread one needed to produce grain ....

Which was where the Wiltshire Horn proved so valuable. Its characteristic meat and wool, neither of them plentiful, might have been considered deficiencies in other breeds; not so, in an animal which was an essential element in the Water Meadow system. It was not overladen with meat or fleece; not heavy enough to damage the edges of the ditches and drawns, or to flatten the beds of the water meadows where it must feed during the barren months; yet still heavy enough to compact the soil of the arable fields needing its manure for grain production.

The Water Meadow Year

The annual cycle of activity on the water meadows took place with the same regularity as religious festivals, beginning in the early autumn. Every drain, drawn and carrier must be scraped free of the silt accumulated during past months. Wooden linings for ditches of all kinds must be inspected and strengthened or replaced where necessary. Hatches must be repaired or replaced. The beds had probably become misshapen after so much flooding and so many hooves; they must be restored. The whole process was known as "Righting up the Works", and all must be completed by Michaelmas when the river water was, in the drowner's opinion, "thick and good". Then, the sluices were opened and the clean meadows had their first drowning of the season; not just for feeding and moisturising. The beds, in being re-shaped, had had the soil loosened, and the drowning helped to compact it again. Thomas Davis expected these drownings to last for two or three weeks at a time, with a couple of days between for a quick draining. Then, no more drowning until grass began to grow, and its roots were established. This was the great advantage of South Wiltshire subsoil – so very porous that the land could really dry quickly, minimising the possibility of stagnation. Even so, constant vigilance was necessary. Forecasting was perilous: "Some meadows that will bear the water three weeks in October, November or December will perhaps not bear it a week in February or March, and sometimes scarcely two days in April or May."

So the work went on through autumn and winter; hatches

open, hatches closed; watch for scum, be alert for signs of frost, when the warm chalky water would protect and feed those precious shoots. Then, towards March, three weeks' drying; the ground firm enough to bear all those sheep, and fresh grass ready to give them the best possible food in the worst possible months.

In this also the Wiltshire Horn sheep proved its value,for it had a habit of holding its dung all day. Ewes and their lambs would walk to the water meadows, feed on that tender grass, and return to their fold on the arable fields later in the afternoon. Not until then would they drop any dung – just where it was needed. The shepherd had to keep watch but there were few accidents; not that he had a sinecure, for as flocks and shepherds were communal, and the minimum number of couples (ewe plus lamb) per acre was five hundred, vigilance was the watchword. Even so, the water meadows were of such size that by the time so many sheep had eaten all the new grass, their normal pasture was ready, and they went to it while a quick drowning - only two or three days – took place. Then the meadows were "laid up" for the hay crop to develop. In six weeks it was ready for cutting; tender, perfect feed for ewes and dairy cows. In years when hay was scarce, a second crop might be sown, but it was sometimes difficult to dry. In any case, cows could be grazed on the water meadows from then until the whole cycle recommenced in the early autumn.

A sceptic asked Davis why water meadows were practically indispensable in South Wiltshire yet "neither used nor missed in other counties." In spite of his misconception, he received a reply which is worth repetition:

> In that month, which so often ruins the crops and exhausts the pockets of those sheep-breeding farmers who have no water meadows, the water meadow farmers may be truly said to be "in clover". They hain up their dry meadows early, so as almost to ensure an early crop of hay; they get their turnips fed off in time to sow barley, and have the vast advantage of a rich fold to manure it. They save a month's hay, and have no occasion to touch their field grass till there is a good bite for their sheep, and their lambs are as forward at May-day as those of their less lucky neighbours at midsummer. And after all they are almost certain of a crop of hay on their water meadows, let the season be what it will.

Disused Water Meadows on River Kennet at Manton

Disused Water Meadows on River Kennet at Manton

The Demise of Water Meadows

Why did the system disappear? The few still surviving are regarded more as historical relics than as economically viable units.

In the post-Napoleonic depression the village cloth trade died; villagers migrated to towns where the hated machines were installed in factories. The Corn Laws were repealed, and locally grown crops were in less demand. Rapaciousness reared its greedy head in trying to improve the Wiltshire Horn breed, and by the 1820s it had been crossed and re-crossed and improved out of all recognition. The Hampshire Down was better in wool and carcass; less good in manure, but that was no longer of any consequence.

There was also the development of mechanisation on the land. The delicate intricacy of a water meadow would respond ungratefully to any machine-driven haymaking; the alternative manual labour if obtainable at all would be prohibitively expensive.

One small point remains. Rowland Vaughan's family were distantly related to the Herberts - a connection formed over two hundred years before Rowland's birth, at the time of Agincourt. In Rowland's time, the Herberts were Earls of Pembroke, created by Queen Elizabeth's young brother, Edward the Sixth. Herberts and Vaughans, bonny fighters all – had they been in Ireland together, or had they formed a friendship at Court?

It so happens that Rowland's book is dedicated to "My good Lord of Pembroke". Had there been some brief hint in a long-forgotten conversation - something taking root, but hidden, until surfacing as new at that moment when the waterprill gave Rowland his new impetus? Because the country seat of the Pembroke family had, since 1551, been at Wilton, in the ancient Wiltshire water meadow country – perhaps those meadows were much older than anyone realised.

In Wiltshire Record Office there is a set of documents dated 1665; they are agreements drawn up between landowners and farmers about the arrangement of water meadows using the River Avon to various farms in the Downton area. It is obvious from these papers that the system was already well established; there was complete understanding of the complicated arrangement of dates and stages in the watering process. Landowners, farmers and lawyers were all well accustomed to the process; it was as normal a procedure as a will or the conveyance of property.

Detailed tables set out the rights and obligations of every person concerned. Between five farmers, according to the area owned, the tables state the stems (periods of time allowed for the use of the water) appropriate to each one; the date of the commencement of each watering, and how many days each user is entitled to have; and so on, through five rounds of watering, until the spring. It was all precise, smoothly-running, with the ease born of very long experience. More than ever, it seems probable that Rowland Vaughan's great idea sprang from some long-forgotten conversation with his Wilton relation, his good Lord of Pembroke.

Plank bridge across a drain near Codford St.Mary in the Wylye Valley

WHITE HORSES

WHITE HORSES

White horses always accompanied Cyrus the Persian on his military expeditions. They were sacred animals, ensuring success, even when advancing upon so powerful a city as Babylon. He set out in springtime, when rivers were swollen by melting snow from the mountains; the most torrential could be crossed only by boat. One of the sacred white horses became restive, pranced in, and was swept away:

> Cyrus, enraged at the insolence of the river, threatened so to break its strength that in future even women should cross it easily without wetting their knees. Accordingly he put off for a time his attack on Babylon, and, dividing his army into two parts, he marked out by ropes one hundred and eighty trenches on each side leading off in all directions, and setting his army to dig, some on one side, some on the other, he accomplished his threat.

White Horses and Water Meadows, five and a half centuries B.C.

Wiltshire is the ideal stable for the other kind of white horses; those animals cut out of the turf on the wide chalk downs, and visible for miles across the valleys. They are too young to be sacred; some of the Celtic and Germanic immigrant people are said to have venerated certain horses, but they arrived in Britain during the millennium before Christ, whereas most of the eleven known Wiltshire horses belong only to the eighteenth or nineteenth centuries.

Another Disappearing White Horse

It is unsafe to state a precise number of Wiltshire white horses. Three of those recorded have disappeared, overgrown by weeds, and another appears and disappears according to the season. When the latter was first officially discovered, it was given the title Albus Equus Redivivus - rather grandiose for a mere part-timer, but it aroused considerable interest at home and abroad.

It appeared in 1948 during ploughing on Rockley Down. Sheep had grazed there for many years, and shepherds had noticed vague marks during exceptionally dry seasons. After ploughing, the old chalk surface was uncovered, and the horse became clear; similar in style to the rest of the eighteenth and nineteenth century breed, and of average size – a hundred and twenty six feet long, nose to tail. It would have been visible to people using the old Swindon to Marlborough road, though not so easily from the A345. Two aerial photographs were taken at the time; a wise precaution, for the horse annually became invisible as the corn covered it yet again. Neither is regular ploughing a process which any White Horse may be expected to withstand indefinitely.

The interest at the time of its discovery reached the overseas press, with the usual legends about it having been cut to commemorate a battle. The only likely battle was the bloodless variety; that of keeping up with the neighbours in adding to the rash of White Horses in that locality. The descendants of that horse's originator were less interested; Plenderleath, the nineteenth century expert on hill figures, knew nothing of it; even in his time it was overgrown.

Uffington's Neighbours

All the Wiltshire Horses but one were in the Marlborough-Pewsey area; all but one were comparatively youthful. By far the most beautiful and ancient of all White Horses is just across the county boundary, in Berkshire: Uffington, a miracle of grace and mystery, which may well have been cut over a thousand years B.C.

That odd horse out in Wiltshire is further south – a useful nag, on Bratton Down; Westbury White Horse. Neither it nor any of its compatriots follow the soaring rapture of Uffington; contemporary taste preferred the realistic hack, and the breed proved numerous.

The Westbury Controversy

Their model was cut on Bratton Down in 1778, completely covering another animal which had for many years been known as Westbury White Horse; reputed to be a squat, ungainly creature with a reptilian tail.

The landowner was Lord Abingdon, and his steward, Mr Gee (sic) supervised the work, presumably on his employer's instructions. Yet the unfortunate Gee has been termed a wretch, vandal, barbarian, miserable being, ignorant destroyer .... What had he done?

"Ignorant destroyer" ought surely to apply to the master as much as to the man, but what had he destroyed? Local tradition said that the original horse been carved on the hillside by King Alfred after defeating the Danes at Edington. His victories over those warriors were always lengthy and exhausting, with heavy casualties. There was no need to set his survivors to work on hillcarving as an alternative to rape and pillage; his men were in their home country, newly freed from the Danes' excesses. They would clear the battlefield, tend the wounded, round up the prisoners; there was the little matter of Guthrum's diplomatic Christianity; hill-carving was low on the list.

Local inhabitants were differently placed. Long deprived of food and safety; the dark winter of fear, with Alfred in hiding, still sharp in the memory; now – the terror vanquished. The King must forge ahead, but his people did the same as the survivors of twentieth century wars. They put up a memorial.

It was not a Christian sign; they were comparatively recent Christians. Their reaction went far deeper, into a millennium of invasion and attack unknown to modern Englishmen. The sacred emblem most deeply etched in their hearts, common to many of the cultures contributing to their history, was the white horse. They etched it deeply into the hillside. Not a king's white charger, nor the fleet enchantment of an unknown genius at Uffington; but a horse, companionable, invaluable, a symbol of security.

It was the antithesis of Uffington; its ordinariness dissociated it from the sense of antiquity as generally understood. Antiquity was shrouded in mystery; perhaps a little battered. Wiltshiremen had Stonehenge, Avebury, and a clear view of Berkshire's Uffington. The Westbury Horse, regularly scoured, was not much noticed by

Westbury White Horse: view with junk

Westbury White Horse: view with picnickers across Vale of West Wiltshire

Westbury White Horse: detail of eye

visitors, antiquaries included. Antiquity was even useful at times; whoever gathered all those sarsens and bluestones provided a handy pool of building material. Westbury Horse was a memorial, nothing more, though associated with so great a king. Leland missed it; so did Defoe, who was in the area in 1685 and again in 1705 without comment.

In 1725, in his "Tour" he wrote of the Vale of the White Horse between Marlborough and Abington (Abingdon). That Vale, and White Horse Hill, had been so called since the Middle Ages and long before; a manuscript in the library of Corpus Christi College rates Uffington White Horse with Stonehenge as one of the wonders of Britain, though it (the manuscript) dates only from the fourteenth century.

Defoe had obviously climbed the hill for a closer examination. He found that the lines of the horse were actually trenches – "about a yard long, and filled almost up with chalk." Then he found that from many miles off, "you see the exact shape of a white horse .... not ill-shap'd I assure you." The wonder in his voice is still plain to hear.

The trench description, applied to the Uffington horse, is appropriate. The figure consists of a series of trenches, curved and arranged with such artistry that they form, as Defoe said, the exact shape of a horse. Yet it has been suggested that he was referring to Westbury White Horse; that the latter was an outline figure.

There was no such suggestion from the Revd Francis Wise, who in 1742 questioned sundry Westbury folk about the date of their horse's creation; he gathered that it had been "wrought within the memory of persons now living or but lately dead." The Revd Wise realised that they might well be confusing the actual making of the horse with the regular communal bustle of scouring which took place about once every seven years. He recorded his findings "with the qualifying suggestion that further enquiry might be desirable."

In 1772 came Gough, editor of *Camden's Britannica*; a literary man, but no artist. He came during the age of the determined amateur; accomplishments were pursued with varying success. Conventionally, one modestly admitted to singing – a little; one played an instrument – a little; gentlemen were spared embroidery, but sometimes sketched – a little; like Mr Gough.

And he sketched Westbury White Horse.

It was definitely from memory, probably some time after his Westbury visit; on one of his less accomplished days. To confirm this, examine the picture of the original White Horse which John Andrews included in his map of Wiltshire in 1773. The map was based upon an original survey; Andrews and his partner, Dury, surveyors both, carried it out together, therefore their horse is less likely to be a hasty imaginative scribble. "We know there is a horse at that spot therefore we have drawn one – details are unimportant." Not in this case. Two men in collaboration tend to be mutually corrective, human nature being what it is. They both saw that hillside during the surveying process. The horse faced towards Edington, as might be expected. It had a sturdy body, but slender legs, and it seemed to be moving forward, flicking its tail. The overall effect was graceful. Its accuracy may be assumed, for the map was intended for the nobility and gentry of the county, of whom eighty, as subscribers, paid for its production. Whilst they may not have quarrelled with any highly technical point of cartography, someone must have noticed an inaccuracy in the appearance or direction of a simple hill figure with which they were all familiar.

Gough's steed, facing in the opposite direction, resembled a dachshund of mallard ancestry. The heavy body was close to the ground, supported by four brief stumps without hooves. The tail was a reptilian specimen bearing no relation to horsehair, tipped by a tiny crescent like a drake's tail feather. It was more a doodle than a sketch; but then, like a small child, Gough achieved one recognisable feature within an impossible whole. He caught the perky lift of the ears. Those of the Andrews and Dury horse are delightfully pricked up as though he heard his master calling; Gough's likewise, though the eye is sliding into space, across the upper edge of the face. Even so, from those ears one must conclude that Gough, Andrews and Dury had seen the same horse.

Astonishingly, Gough remained unchallenged. With at least 176 sets of the Andrews and Dury map sold, no one, during the five years still remaining before Mr Gee began work, compared the two versions of the old horse. After a century, when Plenderleath was writing as an authority in hill figures, he accepted Gough as accurate, ignoring the picture on the map. So did Marples in 1949, and both found reasons for the oddities of the sketch.

It was facing the wrong way? – the engraver had forgotten to reverse the block before printing. It was facing the right way? – its size had rendered Mr Gee's task simple; he had only to superimpose his own much larger animal, and nothing visible remained of the older horse. That crescent at the tip of the imaginative tail? – an ancient symbol of great religious significance.

Still accepting the sketch as a true representation of the earlier horse, Marples asked: Was so strange a horse a relic of antiquity at all? - of course not; it was a great practical joke, a folly, built in the age of follies. This, despite the absence of any record of what must have been a fairly recent and expensive project well within public memory when Gough was writing. If anyone built a mock temple beside a lake in private grounds, publicity would be optional; if they carved a horse out of a hillside visible from miles away, it would be inevitable.

There is also the point that the age of follies was the age of elegance; no one, even the most imaginative, could invest the sketch with that quality. Gough might have enjoyed the joke, had he been around to see the experts taking it so seriously. Neither appears to have read his description, written in Britannica: "a horse in walking attitude."

Andrews and Dury's horse, yes; his own sketch, no. Then, he proves his own habit of superficial, cursory glances, not only in examining hill figures, but in reading about them. He had been reading Francis Wise:

> I am surprised this very learned investigator of these kind of monuments among us should doubt the antiquity of this horse, which so exactly corresponds with the other (Uffington) .... and represent it as of modern make within memory. As I could find no such tradition when I surveyed it in 1772 he must have been misled to confound the scouring as they call it with the original making.

But Wise, in stating his findings, made the clear proviso: "further enquiry might be desirable." And Gough's memory must have failed him completely if he felt able to say that his sketch or its original corresponded exactly with the Uffington figure, in age or appearance.

Whatever the facts, Mr Gee appeared in 1778, presumably with the proper authority, and remodelled the Westbury horse; it seems that his version lacked grace, but subsequent scourings and occasional recutting have provided firm edging, with gratings to drain surplus rainwater. This used to wash chalk from the figure and down the hillside, elongating the legs; an advantage, had the Gough version ever been genuine, but not with the figure as it is. By degrees, the shape changed for the better; the pleasurable lift of the ears has disappeared, but otherwise the horse is pleasing in its utilitarian way.

Pleasing enough to be imitated nine times over.

Cherhill White Horse

This was the first. It appeared in 1780, designed and organised by Dr.Christopher Allsop. He was a prominent resident of Calne; whether his nickname "The Mad Doctor" came before or after his White Horse venture is uncertain. He was also an amateur engineer, and he lived to be eighty-four, so there was plenty of scope either way.

Perhaps he was among those who disliked Mr Gee's efforts, or he may only have felt that what Westbury had, Calne must have in more pleasing form. In his day, a doctor needed to be a good judge of horseflesh, and certainly his White Horse is attractive; well proportioned and graceful. The ears are pricked up - unlike the Gee model, but Dr Allsop must have known its predecessor for many years; the hooves are beautifully shaped, and the animal is trotting. It was cut on the side of a steep earthwork, Oldbury Down, about three miles east of Calne, near Cherhill village; clearly visible from the London road alongside the earthwork.

The Mad Doctor-cum-engineer was also an artist. He marked the outline on the hillside with pegs bearing small flags – no small feat at so steep at angle – then he retreated to a spot from which he could see the horse as passers-by would see it; about two hundred yards away. Some writers have said that he stood on a hill called Labour-in-vain, but that would have been too far away for his purposes. A team of helpers waited beside the horse, and adjusted the pegs as the Doctor directed by signals, and shouting through a speaking trumpet. It must have been exhausting, but a perfect outline was achieved.

Cherhill White Horse

When the cutting was finished, the eye was inlaid with bottles embedded upside down so that the sunlight twinkled on the bottoms. It was a pleasing touch, but short lived. Predatory tourists are not peculiar to the twentieth century.

There were drainage troubles. On that steep slope, even a light shower sent chalk streaming downwards - Plenderleath commented upon the five or six legs, each about three hundred feet long, which tended to appear at such times. Eventually this was ameliorated by a trench cut above the figure, deflecting the worst of the flow.

The Mad Engineer left his ingenious mark on the periodical scouring; chalk was dug a few yards over the brow of the hill, out of sight; it was let down to the horse in little trucks by a windlass. It usually took three men about a fortnight. In 1876 it took a little longer; the rope broke, and one of the trucks missed a workman by the narrowest of margins as it hurtled down the slope.

Long after his demise, Dr Allsop's efforts were appreciated by local people. They gave the horse regular care, and experimented until they found the best way to keep it in good shape. The chalk layer was adjusted; from being six inches below the turf at the upper edges, it was gradually increased until, at the lower extremities, it was banked, with wattle supports to keep the banks in place.

In common with all hill figures, it was camouflaged in 1939; roofing felt, gorse, and wire netting hid the landmark from aerial observation until the war ended.

Pewsey the First, and Alton Barnes

These two were both cut by Robert Pile, a farmer of Alton Barnes, and he encountered so many difficulties that a lesser man would have lost interest.

He cut the first horse in 1785 on Pewsey Hill, about a mile to the south of the village; presumably he had permission from the landowner. If folk memory is to be trusted, it was small – about forty-three feet long - and it had a rider. The cutting seems to have been achieved without trouble, but Robert Pile, in giving his village its own White Horse, expected to follow the custom which had been observed at Uffington from time immemorial. Scouring, necessary every six or seven years, was a communal festival; the people did the work and the landowner provided food and beer. A good time was had by all; all except Mr Pile's landowner.

Whether he objected to the expense or the jollifications, no one knows; but he expressly forbade any repetition. The horse soon disappeared beneath encroaching vegetation. Vague traces have been noticed during very dry weather, as at Rockley, but the rider, if he ever existed, has gone entirely.

Nothing more was attempted until 1812. Mr Pile, still at Manor Farm, was employing a man to do some odd jobs around the farmhouse. John Thorne, usually known as Jack the Painter, generally worked for the Rector of Pewsey, which probably led Mr Pile to assume reliability. Jack was certainly talented; he made a sketch of a white horse which rekindled Mr Pile's old enthusiasm, and when Thorne offered to mark out and cut the horse on Mr Pile's own land, the very considerable sum of twenty pounds changed hands without question. The cutting was to be one foot deep, and filled with chalk.

Thorne disappeared from the district with the money, though he did pause long enough to leave instructions for another man to do the work. Even so, Mr Pile went ahead, and the horse is still a landmark, about five miles from his first attempt. According to Plenderleath it is visible from the spire of Salisbury Cathedral. The villagers have taken good care of it, so that its maker's perseverence has had a lasting and pleasing effect.

Alton Barnes White Horse

Marlborough White Horse: with five legs ?

Marlborough or Preshute White Horse

This is "The Little Horse", and it was cut by schoolboys in 1804. Their school was in Marlborough; Mr Gresley's establishment, not the great school which did not come into existence until 1843.

In planning the project, he found much that was of educational value; mathematics, local and ancient history, art, and physical activity to augment the normal quota of games, not to mention an introduction to manual labour which such boys were otherwise unlikely to receive.

They cut it on Granham Hill, and the principal worker was William Canning, whose home was not far away – the Manor House, at Ogbourne St George. The boys enjoyed themselves, not only at the original construction; Mr Gresley's horse was the only one to be scoured annually, and the event was accompanied by Uffington-type festivities; thanks, no doubt, to the school cook.

The pleasant custom was brought to an end by Mr Gresley's death, and the horse deteriorated rapidly, until, in 1873, an old boy took charge. Captain Reed had been among the boys who cut it in 1804; an elderly gentleman, he cherished happy memories of his schooldays. He organised a complete repair, and it still prances on the hillside.

Hackpen White Horse

Hackpen, or Broad Hinton, or Winterbourne Bassett; take your choice. This horse, larger than Marlborough but still only about ninety feet each way, was cut in 1838 by Henry Eatwell, a parish clerk. It was the year of Queen Victoria's coronation; as good an excuse as any for the villages of Broad Hinton and Winterbourne Bassett to acquire their own White Horse on Hackpen Hill. It was just across the Avebury road, giving all the inhabitants a good view. Hackpen was a steep hill, and chalk drift was a problem. It was kept well in check; the experience of the White Horse pioneers was very valuable. When the 1939 war arrived, Hackpen Hill had a clear, well-shaped White Horse to be camouflaged.

Broad Town

Broad Town, or Wootton Bassett – it is easy to confuse this, the most northerly of all the Wiltshire White Horses, with the previous one. Nearer to Broad Town than Wootton Bassett, it was half a mile to the north-east of the village, on the left of the Wootton Bassett-Marlborough road. Farmer Simmonds of Littleton Farm cut it on his own land in 1863, and he made it very small. He said - possibly tongue in cheek – that he intended to increase its size gradually, making it grow as horses normally do. However, it remained static, and deteriorated somewhat; but by 1939 it was still clear enough to need a covering of hedge cuttings, soil and turf.

View along the escarpment from Broad Town White Horse. The dark bank in the left foreground denotes the 2-3 feet edge of the horse

Devizes: and Ham Hill, or Inkpen

These are no longer with us; both were created in a sudden surge of enthusiasm, and then left to decay.

Devizes Horse was also known as the Snobs' Horse, having been made by the shoemakers of the town. Shoemakers, cobblers – all were commonly known as snobs, a vernacular term used in various parts of the country. In 1845, the snobs of Devizes seem to have had a Whitsuntide outing. They climbed Roundway Hill, and cut a horse just below the point known as Oliver's Camp. It was a hasty creation, and the cutting was of the most perfunctory kind. The snobs' interest departed as quickly as it had come, and the horse was not long in following. When Plenderleath wrote of it in 1874, the traces were very slight – the grass was a different shade during very dry weather – but there was nothing more.

The Inkpen Horse was a similar case. A Mr Wright bought Ham Spray House, from which there was a good view of Ham Hill. This was during the 1860s. He decided to have his own personal White Horse, cut on Ham Hill (had it really been on Inkpen Hill it would have been in Berkshire).

In a short time, Mr Wright left the district. His horse had been only a superficial piece of work, and the new resident was not interested. The horse is only a memory.

1. Uffington White Horse
2. Westbury White Horse
3. Westbury White Horse according to Gough
4. Pewsey White Horse
5. Cherhill White Horse
6 and 7. Ancient British Coins

Illustration from the Rev. Plenderleath's White Horses of Wiltshire and its Neighbourhood in Wiltshire Archaeological Magazine, 1874

Pewsey the Second

In 1937, Pewsey appointed a committee to decide how best to celebrate the coronation of King George and Queen Elizabeth. Every other town and village seemed to be organising bonfires, but Pewsey wished to be different. Why not restore the old White Horse? An expert on the subject, George Marples, was in the area, seeking traces of that same figure, and the committee asked him to help. Traces were there, but scanty; also, it seemed that a higher position might be preferable. They agreed to cut a new one, and Mr Marples submitted three designs. One trotted to the left; one stood, facing left; one, jumping to the right, was complete with a boy rider. Though attractive, the latter would have been a problem to cut, and worse to maintain, even though it recalled the rider on the original horse.

The first design was chosen, and the work was completed by the local fire brigade in a few weeks; placed above the old horse and slightly to the left. Mr Marples, knowing the difficulties of dating hill figures, added the date – 1937 – in clear figures above the horse.

It was very successful; the horse was floodlit, and above it were the initials G:E in flashing red lights. The plan had been to have these illuminations every night for coronation week; two nights were spoilt by thick fog, but the rest were eminently satisfactory.

Footnote

Eleven White Horses have been mentioned; but considering those which have come and gone, others which may have been, but were completely forgotten, and the part-timer, one cannot claim to have been comprehensive. A century ago, the Reverend Plenderleath said much the same thing:

Finality is a thing which cannot, I fear, be predicated of any branch of human knowledge. And I have even heard of persons so depraved as to say that whenever an unusually positive assertion is made .... the only thing of which we may be sure is that the exact reverse will be asserted with equal positiveness a little later.

To that, I will add nothing. Not even one extra White Horse.

Pewsey White Horse

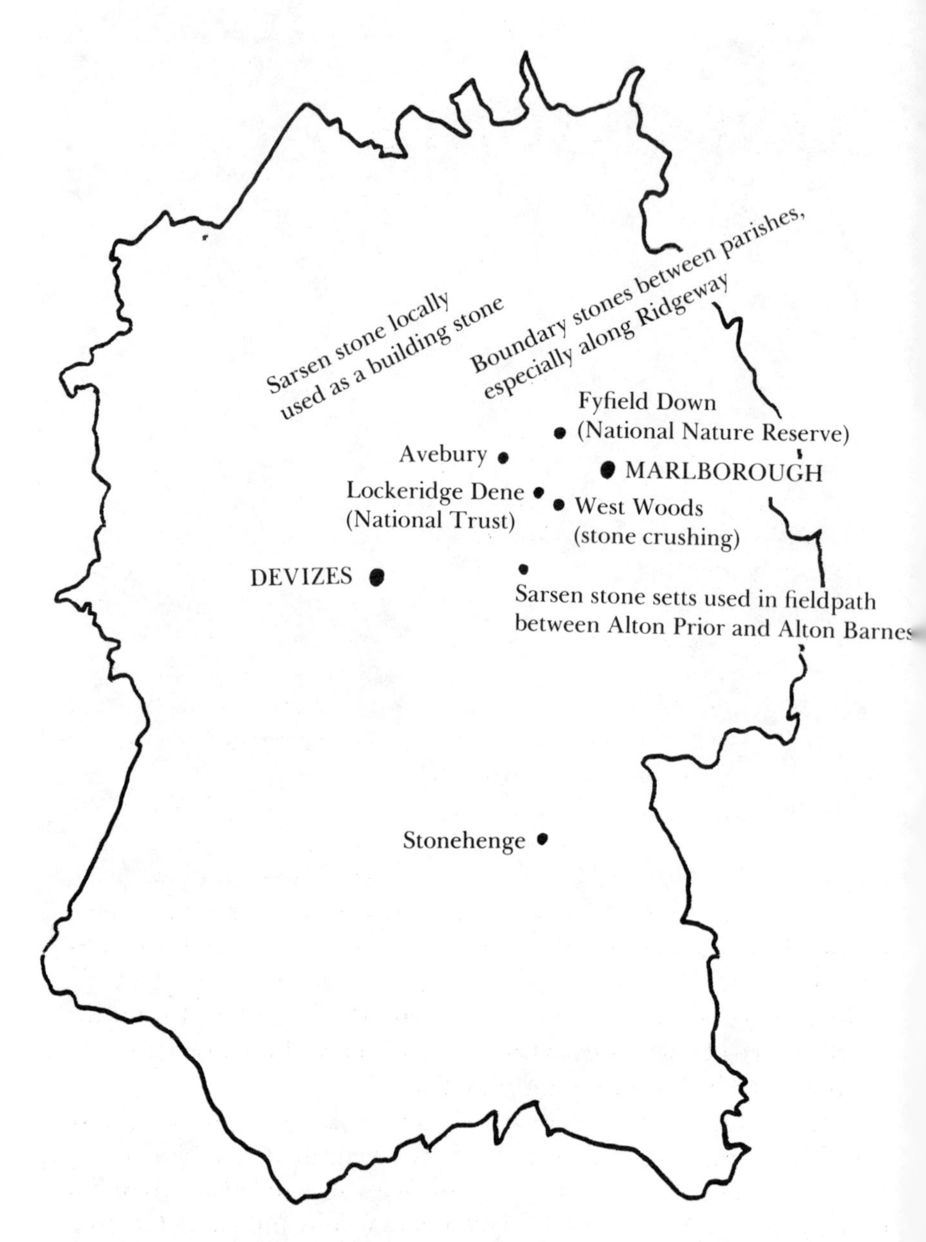

SARSEN STONES are plentiful on the Marlborough Downs and in the Kennet Valley but hardly any are to be seen on Salisbury Plain

SARSEN STONES

Long ago, even by geological standards, great areas of sand covered the chalk which has always been an important component of the Wiltshire landscape. Silica bound those sand grains; a gradual hardening took place, and enormous blocks of sandstone formed. As the process continued, the few disturbances were by water, which flooded away the softer surrounding soil, so that the stones were moved not only by environmental motion but by their own great weight; also by frost which had a similar effect, as did those unlikely but mighty midgets, the worms.

The end product was sarsen stone; very hard, indeed one of the most durable of rocks, and extremely heavy. One cubic foot weighs one hundred and fifty pounds. It occurs across England from Somerset to Kent, from Suffolk to the south coast, and across the Channel around Dieppe, though there is no sign of it on the chalky ground of the Isle of Wight. The main deposits are now in Wiltshire, where distribution is uneven. Though plentiful on the Marlborough Downs and in the Kennet Valley, there are comparatively few to be seen on Salisbury Plain.

A thousand years ago, the Hughenden valley in Buckinghamshire had a vast deposit of sarsens. Then William of Normandy found that his conquest was to be a more protracted affair than our curt phrase "1066, Battle of Hastings" would indicate. His new subjects were reluctant and belligerent; on occasion it was he who needed protection from them. The Hughenden sarsens were put to use. They were plentiful enough to build much of Windsor

Castle; a stern reminder of William's power, and as sturdy a fortress as any unwelcome invader could desire, but it took a heavy toll in Hughenden; sarsens were still there, but in much reduced quantity.

Several millennia before the advent of that conqueror, the islanders had appreciated the natural grandeur of the stones; in Wiltshire Avebury and Stonehenge came into being. The mystery of how, when and why is unlikely to be solved, but the majesty of those monuments is undisputed. Erect or flat, grouped or solitary, split or unbroken, there is an aura of mystery and sombre beauty, partly owing to their impenetrable history, but also to their own attractive qualities.

They are surprisingly colourful, varying from white to autumnal brown, grey and pink - even striped. Frequently, the stripes are brown, indicating a fault in the stone. Such faults go right through, and the stone breaks easily along them; some have split without being touched.

Orange stripes occur when sarsens have been split, shaped and used for building. The stone is not compatible with ordinary cement; any joining must be done with lime mortar, which attracts orange and yellow lichens, making an attractive contrast to the darker surface of weathered sarsen. Whatever the surface colour, the grains of sand forming the stone always catch stray sunbeams; weathered, immeasurably ancient, yet momentarily a sarsen gives the same thrill of pleasure as a sparkling Christmas tree.

Other than Sarsen, the stones have a variety of names; the Buckinghamshire variety was known as Denver Hill. Saracen probably came into use when the descendants of William of Normandy were crusaders in the Holy Land, battling against the Saracens who were not only infidels but magicians, necromancers .... and what but magical powers could have lifted those great stones into position? Saracen stones they must be.

Men of a later, more pastoral age, looked across the wide Wiltshire hillsides and saw flocks of grey-fleeced sheep lying in groups .... yet they never moved, even to graze. Smaller grey sarsens, from a distance, bear a remarkably close resemblance to sheep; Grey Wethers – though this name is shared with a group of stones on Sittaford Tor, Dartmoor; they also resemble sheep from a distance, but they are granite.

Sarsens by the roadside between Broad Hinton and Rockley

Local dialect provided slight variations on the general name; sarsdon, sarsden, sassen, saeson – whatever the colour, the name, or the district, the stone cast its spell upon all who saw it, or worked with it. Aubrey wrote, impressively: "Many of them are mighty great ones, and particularly those in Overton Wood."

Brentnall, writing at the end of the second world war, continued that observation: "The sarsens there (Overton Wood) had lighter coloured rinds than we are used to see on the open downs, and formed in Spring a perfect background for the bluebells that grow in such vertiginous profusion below the oaks and birches." He added sadly, "The stones are gone for the most part to make the roads of Swindon."

They fascinated him. "The true sarsen is handsome within," and, having seen the mason preparing one for use, "the almost dazzling cubes lying in even rows .... beside a snowy heap of dust and fragments."

Use and misuse

Men of the Palaeolithic age used hand axes of stone; many were flint, made by the flaking process. By the Neolithic age, agriculture and animal husbandry augmented the uncertain provision of the hunter's life; sarsen was an ideal stone for grinding and pounding.

Imagination was needed to make those small tools; imagination, activated by the need to survive. The use by the same people of the great monoliths shows imagination of another kind. When their leaders or otherwise eminent people died, there was a desire to provide a fitting tomb. No simple hole in the ground; a place of peace and dignity, apparently intended for use as a shrine.

They constructed tomb chambers; long barrows, supported internally by sarsen monoliths, with entrances having posts and lintels of the same rough grandeur. The stonework was covered by earth mounds so firmly built that they remained unmoved for thousands of years. Such was the engineering ability of those early men; the initial planning, the organisation, and the achievement.

It was a natural progression from the use of sarsen monoliths as monumental protection for the dead, to their use in the service of the living. We can never know exactly how it was done, but the mechanics of moving, lifting and positioning were learned laboriously through unnumbered years. Such lessons could not be learned without heavy cost - one suspects the use of slave labour, or some similarly expendable work force.

This may well have been drawn from the indigenous population; immigration from the Continent was comparatively frequent. Spain, Brittany, Germany, Crete – the immigrants were intrepid travellers, and came to an island already having a network of tracks developed since prehistoric times, focussing on the ancient Ridgeway, a prehistoric M4. They brought with them knowledge from their own stone cultures, and found an existing expertise. They also brought bronze – an advance which must have given them the advantage.

Whatever the methods, no matter who were the overlords, the skills acquired were applied to a new purpose. Sarsen circles were formed; some small, others larger, culminating in the intricate majesty of Avebury. Whether they were intended as meeting places, temples, or settings for royal pomp, they were erected by accomplished engineers. Whatever their original purpose, they

Upended sarsen at Avebury

Stonehenge: "The Mysterious Made Mundane"

now remain as works of art. Like other such works, they have suffered periods of neglect, of non-recognition; like the others, they are capable of many different interpretations.

Stonehenge, younger than Avebury, is in the same category; a work of art arousing awe and wonder. Its great stones were brought long distances, though this seems to have been almost run-of-the-mill work - after all, some of the sarsens inside the earlier long barrows of the Marlborough Downs were of a kind occurring twenty miles away, in Somerset. By the time Stonehenge was being planned, transport was possibly not considered the greatest problem.

It was no longer a matter of unworked monoliths; the whole complex as we know it took about thirteen centuries to develop. First came the earthworks and a few sarsens; then, a double circle of bluestones, left incomplete. Possibly their transportation via that tortuous route from the Prescelly Mountains proved too costly in labour and life. About a century later the great sarsen work took place; an early example of those periods of happy fruition seen in later centuries, as when the creative genius of Leonardo and Michaelangelo coincided with the vision and resources of the Medici. Without benefit of written records, the Stonehenge sarsens are chronicles of the co-existence of artistic vision, engineering genius, and command of vast resources.

It was a stupendous creation. Thirty uprights for the main circle, each about twenty-five tons in weight, over thirteen feet high, and seven feet wide. In the inner horseshoe, the five pairs of uprights were graduated in height from over sixteen feet to twenty-two at the centre; another eight feet were needed to sink into the ground, or so dense a stone would never remain upright.

Those great boulders must be sought out, shaped and transported. Lintels of suitable size must similarly be provided; five for the horseshoe, and thirty for the outer circle, every one carefully shaped to maintain the curve. Every upright was tapered a little towards the top; every top surface was dished. A hollow, ground laboriously with a rounded sarsen hammer, leaving a tenon protruding in the middle to fit a corresponding mortice ground in the lintel. Precision work, all of it, achieved on the hardest of stone with primitive tools; a task for experts with the inherited experience of millennia behind them.

To build; to plan, organise and labour, needed many people. The commissariat needed many more. It was a great population, articulate and intelligent, with more years of growth behind them than lie between ourselves and Julius Caesar. Yet the next thousand years brought such decline that memories were erased. The mighty effort and its purpose were forgotten. The sarsens must have been placed at Avebury and Stonehenge by magical means.

Even so, if we move forward to times when magic was genuinely feared, and suspected sorcerers harshly punished, those magical stones were not regarded with much awe. They were free for all; bluestones and sarsens, taken and used for current requirements. Much sarsen went into the making of many an early church in Wiltshire, particularly those in the Avebury area and the Winterbourne valley; cut, uncut, any colour, any size; presumably the sacred nature of the building would destroy any taint of magic.

Many of those churches have stood since Plantagenet times, and remain sturdy enough to stand as long again and more. Contemporary houses were less so; largely built of wood, or occasionally some brick; sarsen would have been too great a drain upon a workforce severely depleted by the Black Death; it served for sacred purposes. Not until the middle of the sixteenth century did builders begin to consider the possibilities. Sarsens were used as lasting foundations for houses in which generation could follow generation; almost a century had passed since the long cut and thrust of the Wars of the Roses; the middle classes and prosperous artisans were putting down roots, as had the aristocracy in their earlier castles. Foundations, floors, ovens, walls, chimneys – the stone houses were often more spacious than the old ones, for the stone was plentiful. One of the Avebury monoliths contained about ninety tons of stone; all there for the breaking and taking, and so the monument was gradually depleted. Fortunately the Grey Wethers were infinitely more numerous, and needed less effort. They lay on Fyfield Down and in Kennet Valley – "full of grey pibble stones of great bignes .... they lie so thick as you may go upon them all the way" – so wrote a Royalist, marching cross-country in 1644. He noticed that people broke the stones roughly to build houses and walls – "laying mosse betweene"; presumably the masons had not yet reached a high standard; it was a very difficult stone to cut evenly. Other disappointments awaited them; sarsen, being so dense, was completely waterproof, therefore when there was any dampness in the atmosphere the stones were wet with condensation. Early in the eighteenth century, William Stukely's view as a householder was distinctly peevish: "damp and unwholesome, and rots the furniture".

A more peaceful anecdote belongs to that period. In 1719, the incumbent of Winterbourne Monkton died, and his grave was marked by a sarsen taken from his own glebe. Clear lettering on that stone would have been near-impossible to achieve, but his parishioners found a more suitable epitaph. He had loved the children of his parish, and for many years acted as their teacher. When some little ones found that letters were hard to learn, Parson Brinsden thought of a way to help them. He planted snowdrops; all the letters of the alphabet were in his garden, marked out in tiny white flowers; what enchantment, in early Spring, to walk in Parson's garden, learning letters from snowdrops. They were his memorial; year after year, the sarsen slab was surrounded by a carpet of dainty blooms, planted by former pupils.

He was a contemporary of the historian Bishop of Salisbury, Gilbert Burnet; another advocate of sugared educational pills, who

Sarsen setts forming a footpath between the villages of Alton Priors and Alton Barnes in the Vale of Pewsey

Sarsen in River Kennet, west of Marlborough

had gentled one of his own sons from teenage rebellion among the Mohocks to later respectability as a man of the cloth. Burnet took great pride in visiting every parish in his diocese; he must have seen John Brinsden's work and delighted in it.

Home-produced, and used in reverence, just as the earliest builders of the long barrows had used theirs – no one could grudge Parson Brinsden his sarsen stone. But only fifty years later, Sir Joseph Banks, Captain Cook's naturalist, noted with some concern that many of the sarsens between Silbury and Marlborough had been broken. Crushed to make roads, broken to make garden walls, cut to shape for gate posts, doorsteps and kerb stones; left uncut outside cottages, to double as protective boulders against passing vehicles, and seats for cottagers - small wonder they were no longer so thick upon the ground. In 1939 four wagon loads of sarsen blocks went from Marlborough to repair walls at Windsor Castle – the Normans had chosen their material wisely. During the world war which began in the following months, other sarsens which had lain on the Wiltshire Downs for many thousands of years, were blown to dust by troops whose need to practise their skills with explosives was undeniable.

Working the Sarsen

At the turn of the century, stone 56 at Stonehenge was tilting dangerously, and there were indications of an imminent break. It was supported in a wooden cradle, and the surrounding soil was excavated, a very small section at a time. Each excavation was refilled with concrete, and the original contents carefully sifted. Chalk, flint, and even the sarsen tools used to shape the boulders - all had been thrown in and hammered down hard to provide sufficient support from the base of the very deep hole. Sarsen hammers, and great rounded mauls; which immediately arouse queries as to the incidence of foot injuries; handling tools of such weight must have exhausted the arms of the most muscular artisan. However, people capable of such feats of engineering probably had their own ingenious preventive procedure.

For any early masons, natural faults, as along the brown stripes, were the obvious places to break the boulders. They assisted the process by hammering wedges into the fault line; otherwise, in the absence of such a line, small wedge holes were laboriously chipped into the stone as required. When enough wedges were in place, a blow from a large hammer did the rest. A suitable weight was about 14lb.

In the seventeenth century an Avebury man, Walter Stretch, found a different method. Mr Stukely of the rotting furniture left a clear description:

> The method is, to dig a pit by the side of the stone, till it falls down, then to burn many loads of straw under it. They draw lines of water along it when heated, and then with smart strokes of a great sledge hammer, its prodigious bulk is divided into many lesser parts. But this Atto da fe (sic) commonly costs thirty shillings in fire and labour, sometimes twice as much. They own too 'tis excessive hard work; for these stones are often 18 feet long, 13 broad, and 6 thick; that their weight crushes the stones in pieces, which they lay under them to make them be hollow for burning; and for the purpose they raise them with timbers of twenty feet long, and more, by the help of twenty men; but often the timbers were rent in pieces.

Mr Stukely took a depressed view of all things sarsen, whether in the making, or the finished product, giving a doleful account of Walter's first effort:

> He exercised this at first on one of the stones standing in the street before the inn, belonging to the outer circle of the southern temple. That one stone, containing twenty loads, built the dining room end of the inn. Since then, Tom Robinson .... made cruel havoc among them. He owned to us that two of them cost £8 in the execution. Farmer Green ruined many of the southern temple to build his houses and walls at Beckhampton.

Nothing to do with those stones was easy, but a cheaper method of firing them evolved. The required line of breakage was heated by fat and twigs; the fire was sustained until the heat was sufficiently great, then the ashes were knocked away, and very cold water dashed across the heated area.

As the stone-breakers saw it, there were excellent reasons for their work. Imagine the bulk of a stone which, when broken, provided material enough to "build the dining room end of the inn;" if left standing in the street before the inn, it must impede the approach of too many vehicles for the innkeeper's peace of mind. How much better to use it as an extension. And there were others, also of great bulk, lying out in supposedly arable fields. Every year, the plough had to work its way around them; it was wasted time, and wasted land. Farmers had tried to solve the problem by sinking the stones; pits at least eight feet deep were made beside the sarsen, and the stone, with much difficulty, edged in. It saved future effort, but "it was reckoned that the cost of sinking them below ploughing level was more than thirty years' purchase of the spot they stood on." How much wiser to fire the stones; initial outlay would be covered by selling it as cheap building material, and the land was freed for agriculture. Destruction of the sarsens may spell desecration to the archaeologist, but to self-supporting country dwellers it was a matter of common sense, and a couple of centuries were to pass before any other view gained ground.

Sarsen blocks with limestone dressings: West Overton Church tower

Grey Wethers at Lockeridge Dene

Sarsen blocks with brick dressings: Firs Cottages at Rockley

Roughly worked sarsen blocks in garden wall at Fyfield

Finely worked sarsen blocks at Marlborough College

As late as 1946, Mr Brentnall recognised this, and also the masons' pride in their tools and their work: "The modern sarsen cutter does not employ the arduous and costly method of burning. Armed with tools of the finest temper, he chips sockets for his wedges in the selected stone, and the heavy sledgehammer wielded by his mate at length divides the mass".

These tools were treasured. Every mason possessed two sets. One, he used; the other was with the blacksmith being serviced, and they were changed every weekend. Nevertheless, Mr Brentnall viewed the results with misgiving and a graphic metaphor: "Those who have watched the district through this century have seen the wolf at work in many a fold of grey wethers, daily devouring apace, and nothing said." He was right, Earlier depredation had been severe but it paled in comparison with that which took place from about 1850.

Hughenden had supported two sarsen masons, the brothers Thomas and Edward Free. Less than two miles away, at High Wycombe, the Cartwrights also worked, but by 1850 none of them could make a living. Sarsen, known there as Denver Hill stone, was present, but mainly below the surface. Labour costs were punitive; the time and energy spent in searching, then raising the stones, used any profit even before the working began. Whereas Wiltshire men had gone to great pains to bury their sarsens, the Hughenden men had to delve as much as thirty feet to obtain theirs.

There was a general exodus. Thomas Free moved to Frenchay, to work Pennant Stone. Edward Free moved to Fyfield, as did the Cartwrights; there was plenty of work for everyone; more, they were near Honeystreet Wharf, on the Kennet and Avon Canal. Loads of stone were taken to Bristol, and the boats returned, laden with coal, which sold easily in the Kennet Valley. Another brother of the Free family ran the necessary adjunct to all this industry – The Fighting Cocks.

It was a boom period. Tramways being built in many towns and cities needed sarsen setts; industrial growth meant new roads – kerbstones, water supply hydrants, gate posts, walls, doorsteps. Great buildings - the exterior of Marlborough College Chapel, a new wing for Marlborough Priory (now a Day Centre); extensive estates of workers' houses; there was plenty of stone for everything. The Frees worked in Fyfield and Lockeridge, and the Kimmers and the Waites, fathers and sons, all skilled masons, worked for them for many years. The Cartwrights worked also in Fyfield, employing the Bristows.

At first all their tools went back to High Wycombe every week for tempering; no one in Wiltshire understood that work. Eventually the West Overton blacksmith was able to take over, saving a considerable amount of time and expense. Each mason needed a two-edged hammer – a pecker – to make the initial cuts, and several were needed, of varying degrees of sharpness, to cut one sarsen. He needed a punch to finish the holes begun with the peckers; wedges for splitting, and the hammer to drive them in. Several other tools were necessary for making setts, and they all made their weekly trip to the blacksmith; a considerable drain on a weekly wage of about £2-5s, which was the approximate rate for a skilled man in the years betwen the wars. If they had the energy, there was usually overtime to be earned, by removing sarsens from farmers' land. But their own work began at 6.30am and there was usually a long walk – two or three miles - to get there in the first place, though they finished at 4pm. Usually they worked high on the downs, and

Edward Free's headstone in Fyfield churchyard

Honey Street wharf on the Kennet and Avon Canal

their only shelter was a rough shield of hazel and thatch, little more than a hurdle, They wore goggles to protect their eyes from the flying splinters of steel, but the backs of their hands betrayed their occupation - they were pitted with tiny blue marks under the skin where the steel had struck.

In 1915, the Cartwrights' mason, Walter Bristow, died. They closed their business and left the district. Since the turn of the century the Frees' annual output had been about 300 tons, and they had six men working for them. Edward Free had died long since, and his son William carried on, followed in turn by his son Douglas. As the twentieth century wore on, the sarsen trade grew less, owing to the increasing use of concrete which was much cheaper, and easier to use. What they lost in that direction the Frees made up in the coal trade. Their last mason, Cecil Waite, found a strange kind of spare-time work for a skilled sarsen cutter: he spent his winters cutting turf for the local parks department.

Saving the Sarsens

Concern had been sporadic and slight; many people saw the case for making use of the sarsens more clearly than the case for preservation. Not until 1907 was any firm move made. Then, the thirteen-year-old National Trust joined forces with the Natural History Society of Marlborough College, and Wiltshire Archaeological Society, in launching an appeal for funds to purchase some areas where sarsen could remain undisturbed. They raised £612, and bought Piggledene and Lockeridge. In 1930 Wiltshire Archaelogical Society decided to do the same for Totterdown; they met at the top of Avebury Down, together with some visitors whose presence was calculated to arouse wider interest. Split sarsens lay glinting in the sunlight; snowy setts lay cut and ready for removal. It was too late.

The National Trust, looking at Piggledene, found that some of the boulders had been split, and decided to cement them together again to restore the original appearance of the area. However, after a few years they found sarsen was impervious to cement; the stones split again.

In one instance, sarsen actually saved itself. In 1920, a partnership set up a stone-crushing plant in West Woods.They broke the sarsens with explosives and put the remnants through a crusher, selling the result for road metalling. Then it was found that the first puff of wind blew it all away, and the purchasers were dissatisfied.

In West Woods, the concrete base of a stone crusher, and the dearth of sarsens, are the only reminders of a bankrupt firm.

Even so, the greatest factor in the preservation of sarsen was probably the growth of the concrete industry; so much easier to shape, to use and to transport – the remaining sarsens may well be undisturbed for many years.

The great monuments were saved by the generosity of private purchasers. Alexander Keiller bought Avebury in 1925; he was a wealthy member of the Society of Antiquaries. By 1942, when the National Trust took over, he had financed much restorative and archaeological work. Now, it is in the hands of the Department of the Environment.

The original owner of the land on which Stonehenge stands was killed in the first world war, together with his heir. In 1915 the property was auctioned, and purchased by another local man for £6600. Three years later he presented it to the nation.

Footnote

Sarsen masons worked high on the hills; open to every wind, every breeze; their only shelter those home-made hurdles. But look at this list:

Edward Free	aged 45
Charles Waite	aged 45
Henry Waite	aged 42
Frank Kimmer	aged 50
Walter Bristow	aged 48

Men in their prime? They should have been; but those were the ages at which they died. Every one was killed by silicosis, that insidious "dust" disease which has killed so many men in deep coal mines. They had all the fresh air denied to miners; yet their lungs were ruined even earlier in life than by coal dust. That hardest of stones was no less tough when reduced to dust; those miniscule specks of steel flew with momentum enough to pierce the back of a mason's hands; some may well have joined the sarsen dust inside the lungs.

How they must have struggled, towards the end. The long climb to work; the heavy labour; and the need for overtime whenever possible. Magic stones, tragic stones . . .

Finely worked sarsen gatepost at Rockley

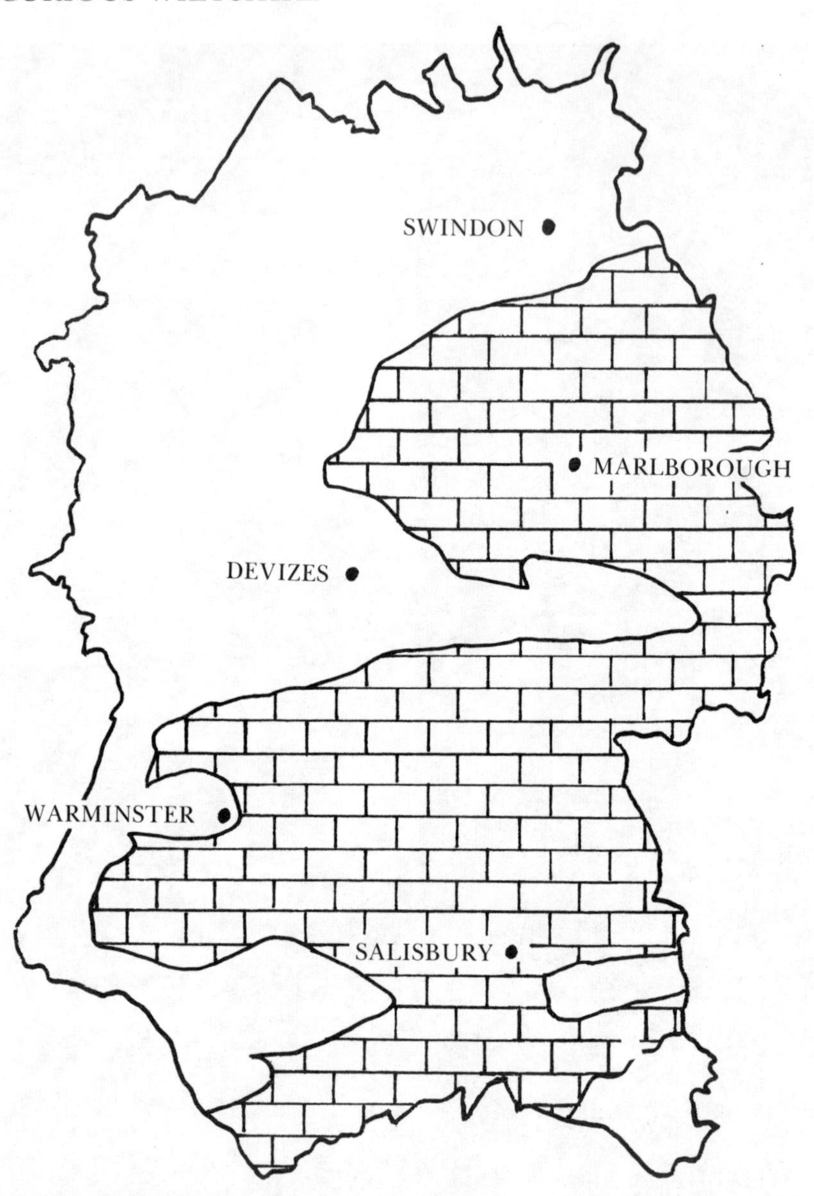

DEW PONDS The map of Wiltshire above shows the covering of chalk in the County, much of which represents upland, notably Salisbury Plain and the Marlborough Downs. Dew ponds no longer function: they have dried up and sometimes been infilled, yet it is still possible to discover one beside a track on the open downs – the regular saucer-like depression in the ground is unmistakeable.

DEW PONDS

> Stars of Morning, dew-drops which the sun
> Impearls on every leaf and every flower

Dew and poetry have long kept company, whether in literary work or folk lore.

> The lark in the morning
> Rises up from her nest.
> She'll mount the white air
> With dew on her breast.

It was useful as well as beautiful; witness the girl with red rosy cheeks and coal-black hair.

> I'm going a-milking
> Kind sir, she answered me -
> It's dabbling in the dew
> Makes the milkmaids fair.

Useful, beautiful and romantic; no wonder dew was so closely associated with sheep ponds, those near-miraculous little oases which meant so much to shepherds.

They occurred only on the heights of the great chalk downs – the summit of the countryman's world. Far from rivers, streams and springs, they rarely failed even in the hardest drought. Wells dried, village ponds became a complication of mud cracks; still the sheep ponds retained water. They had other names, but as far as one can tell, since the early nineteenth century, dew pond was the most widely used.

That great naturalist of the eighteenth century, Gilbert White, knew them in his native Hampshire and also in neighbouring Wiltshire, but appears not to have used the term dew pond: "we have many such little round ponds in this district (Selborne) .... one in particular on our sheep-down, three hundred feet above my house, and containing perhaps not more than two or three hundred hogsheads of water; yet it is never known to fail, though it affords drink for three or four hundred sheep, and for at least twenty head of cattle beside .... By my journal of May 1775 it appears that "the small and even considerable ponds in the vales are now dried up, while the small ponds on the very tops of the hills are but little affected."

Thomas Davis, the agricultural expert writing towards the close of the same century, referred to them as sheep ponds:

> Sheep wells and sheep ponds are objects of great necessity to a tenant, though of expense to a landlord. Wherever ponds can be made, they are much more eligible than wells for watering sheep ....it is a very difficult matter for a farmer to prevent his sheep from having too much water at one time, and too little at another, when they can get no water but what is drawn for them at wells.

Those essential but expensive ponds were still not known as dew ponds, but early in the nineteenth century came increasing scientific interest in the nature of dew. In 1814, Wells proved to his own satisfaction that it descended upon the ground from moisture already in the air.

In 1836 Blythe proved, also to his own satisfaction, that it ascended from the ground, condensing after having risen with the heat from the earth.

Later, Aitken decided that either theory could be correct, given suitable conditions. Then came Edward Martin; clear-thinking, questioning, with a passion for detail, a sense of humour, and an almost life-long interest in dew ponds. By the time he was old enough to realise their existence they were well established as such. It was in about 1880:

> My personal interest was drawn to the subject by my old schoolmaster during a well-remembered walk across the Falmer downs. The statement was made that a pond which was visited on the way was fed entirely by dew. I permitted myself to ask a question mentally as to what became of the rain which fell into it.

What makes a Dew Pond?

Largely, the name; the actual amount of dew deposited is tiny. English people will not be surprised by that; their language has many such perverse expressions. As I write, in cool springtime, I recall the lone blackthorn on a Surrey hillside, gleaming as white as newly-fallen snow. Gilbert White's hogsheads were nothing to do with animals – merely casks. The downlands where dew ponds occur are most definitely uplands. And dew ponds are anything but.

Other names were frequently used; cloud, fog, or mist ponds; even artificial rain ponds – the pond being artificial rather than the rain. Each name refers to one of the several elements of moisture presumed to be present; the people who commonly used them recognised that they were approximate definitions rather than accurate terms. Martin wrote: "As a matter of fact I have spoken with farmers with whom the word "dew pond" is in familiar use, who agree that when they speak of dew they include in that word condensation from mist and clouds also."

He had noticed that shepherds needing a new pond would wait high on the downs as sunrise broke through the banks of haze; when much had disappeared, smaller pockets remained resting in the hollows. In one of those they would site the pond, in a spot which had retained the haze; there, a pond would last.

Earlier in his career Martin wrote in an article: "Summer fogs are very common at night on the high downs, the people who go to bed and get up at normal hours do not know of them. These fogs are so wet that a man riding up on the hills at 4 am may find his clothes wringing wet from the fog, and every tree dripping water ...."

Folk memory recorded the same fact.

I wooed her in the winter time
And in the summer too -
And the only only thing I ever did wrong
Was to shield her from the foggy foggy dew.

Romantic, yet a basic necessity; the stuff of poetry, yet it must be kept in its place. Men going early to work went in dew-beaters; the strongest boots they could afford, and even then stuffed with straw for extra protection. Harvest workers with dew-beaters on their feet hoped for a dew-cap before they began work - a drink of ale to cheer them through the chill grey light before the sun rose.

The word was ubiquitous, and it, with all the other elements thought to fill dew ponds, was taken seriously, particularly by people with a theoretical interest, scientists and amateurs alike. The Government Grant Committee of the Royal Society gave Edward Martin a bursary large enough to enable him to make a three-year study of the subject. His store of knowledge already commanded respect; the enthusiasm he brought to this further study seemed unlimited. It was his great passion in life, the enigma of these remote, apparently miraculous ponds. He can rarely have been at home, except to collect dry clothing and still more of the kitchen utensils he used in his experiments. He sat up all night beside his favourite dew ponds; he constructed an experimental one, then dug it up and started again. Not that he disregarded the absence of creature comforts: "I may remark that a journey over the downs in mid-winter at night-time, with only the stars to guide one, with the thermometer considerably below freezing point, and an icy blast blowing from the north-east, is an experience to remember." Finding the dew in a dew pond was no sybaritic assignment.

What, and why

The construction of a dew pond was a vital factor in determining its moisture content. A mere hollow on the summit of chalk downs would be permeable, with infinite capacity for absorption; no moisture could be retained.

Puddling made a difference. If the chalk were rammed and hammered into a creamy consistency, then smoothed into a cement-like surface, it was watertight. The work was hard, for the rammers must be very heavy, but results were good. However, if that surface were damaged – perforated from beneath by worms burrowing upwards, or strong plants; or broken from above by the sharp cloven hooves of sheep, then the pond would run dry. An old man told Martin of such a pond; in his boyhood the chalk surface sustained damage, and the remaining water was so sparse as to be

Heavy rains foil a farmer's attempts to infill this Dew Pond near Marlborough.

useless – except for one thing. He asked permission to drive his horses through it after work, to clean their hooves. Gradually that pond's water deepened; the hooves had acted as rammers, puddling and repairing the leaks. He could also remember being told to drive oxen round and round the chalk surface of another pond, dragging a broad-wheeled cart behind them. After a day's treatment, the chalk was well puddled, and the faults repaired. The surface, smoothed with spades, was again waterproof.

Natural hollows often needed modification; sometimes the size was inadequate, or the sides sloped at an insufficiently gradual angle. In winter, ice might well cover the surface of the water, and within near-perpendicular sides it would cut the chalk puddling, as ice floes at sea can crush a ship. Given a very gradual slope, the ice had room for safe expansion.

Sometimes, a natural hollow retained a clay lining left from past ages; useful, and efficient in waterproofing, but vulnerable. Worms could thrust upwards and ruin clay puddling, but a mixture of lime with the clay usually discouraged them.

This was all comparatively simple, but Martin met a Wiltshire farmer whose landlord, the Marquess of Aylesbury, included in all his leases conditions regarding the construction of dew ponds. They were elaborate and expensive; no natural hollow was deep enough to accomodate such work:

> Three layers of straw, each three inches in thickness when pressed down, are placed alternately between three layers of puddled clay, the whole series giving a thickness of 2ft.6ins., no other substance being required. The best wheat-straw is used, not cut in any way. The lowest layer is straw, the topmost clay. The ponds are then railed round in order to prevent cattle straying into them .... each pond costs about £300; they are of large size, being about 60 feet across. The pond so made lasts roughly about one hundred years.

In Sussex, straw was used, as a bad conductor of heat; the theory was, that it would hold back the heat normally rising from the earth, therefore the pond water would stay cool.

Martin queried that. Being a bad conductor, the straw would also prevent solar heat from penetrating the earth beneath the water;

Dew Pond on Milk Hill below Alton Barnes White Horse: nettles flourish where livestock once drank

therefore the heat of that water would rise considerably during the day. Yet to produce dew – ie. to condense mist into droplets, the pond must, according to theory, be of a lower temperature than either air or mist. Therefore the straw, if it worked at all, would be self-defeating. However, only dry straw could act in this way, as a poor conductor; damp, soggy, crushed between all those layers of heavy clay which itself had been heavily compressed during the puddling process – it would almost immediately cease to be a barrier to heat, either rising or falling.

Could it be protected from such compression? And what other non-conducting material might be used for its protection? Wood, and fine wood shavings. Martin made his own dew pond. First the usual chalk base, puddled, hammered and smoothed, covered by a thick layer of fine wood shavings. Then came the straw, protected by a slightly raised platform of planks. Puddled clay lay over that, carried in a sweeping curve up the sides of the pond, protecting all that lay below. The whole area was topped by a thick layer of powdered chalk, and surrounded by a fence of wire netting.

It was late autumn, and the pond had a hard time. Heavy rain preceded a winter of heavy snowfalls and severe frost. The water was frozen solid, thrusting with all possible force against the clay bottom and sides. When the frost disappeared, the melting water failed to hold; some wag had thrust a thick stick through the clay. February ended very dry; what with the one-way drainage system and lack of rain, the pond was just a dry hollow, its clay beginning to crack.

Salvation came with an English summer. Water held in the middle, in the area unaffected by the errant walking stick. Martin had just returned home from investigations elsewhere; joyfully, he smoothed the areas still exposed until "they were as smooth as glass."

He had to go away again for a few days, during which a flock of sheep trampled the fence, drank the water, and made a multitude of holes in the clay with their small cloven hooves...."

Less joyfully, he puddled and smoothed the broken clay; he decided to test for dew. A roof of twigs, supported over the pond, was covered with a waterproof sheet. Night One was rainless, and in the morning the underside of the sheet was covered in moisture. Was it dew, or evaporation from the pond? Night Two was also rainless, but moisture lay on the upper side of the sheet.

Surely, that was dew; there had been no cloud from which mist could have been precipitated. Moreover, the quantity was minute. That was the twelth of June; no rain fell between the tenth and the twenty-first. During that rainless period, the pond surface dried into many cracks. If indeed there was any dew, there was too little to have any effect. Then a great storm saturated the ground; cracks disappeared from the pond, and four inches of water lay in the bottom.

Martin re-excavated his pond. As he suspected, the straw was damp and crushed in spite of the attempt to protect it with planks, therefore its insulation value was nil. The contribution of dew to the pond was similar; even when the surrounding grass was heavily laden, there was no increase in pond content; no dew had been added. Either it evaporated or it sank into the ground; it had not trickled down the sloping sides into that pond.

Strangely he seems to have enquired no further into other possible functions of straw in the ponds. Sussex was the centre of all his work - his home, and "the home of the dew pond;" other information reached him from English counties as far away as Yorkshire, and from foreign countries including India and South Africa; it was all of interest, but Sussex and its ways were his focal point.

Even in chatting to the Wiltshire farmer he seems not to have asked why straw was part of that dew pond; so much of his time had been devoted to his own view of it as a cooling agent, as the method of reducing pond temperature to a sufficiently low level to condense mist over its surface. That it might, in other districts, have another purpose, did not occur to him. In his pre-dawn hours on the summit of the downs he had seen clearly that a low pond temperature was not essential for mist condensation; it happened on clothing warm from the body, hence his saturated condition. He also noted the shepherd's admission that "dew" was in common use as a general rather than specific term. Yet still he did not wonder whether straw in pond construction might be used with some intention other than insulation.

The answer was simple. Straw, in a Wiltshire pond, was merely a protective covering. Whether in the elaborate ponds prescribed by the Marquess of Aylesbury, or the less expensive type preferred by Thomas Davis, straw prevented the clay puddling from drying out or being harmed by wandering hooves, before mist condensed and filled it, or the rain fell on centre and sides.

The hollow was lined with a mixture of clay and lime, well rammed and puddled. A thick straw covering delayed evaporation of the moisture content until the pond was filled. A heavy top layer of chalk rubble served the dual purpose of holding the straw in place and discouraging animals from walking across. A small amount of water at the bottom kept the straw moist for the benefit

Overgrown Dew Pond near Sutton Veny (centre foreground)

of that all-important clay surface. A tree or bush was advantageous. Mist condensed on the overhanging leaves and fell into the pond; in particularly heavy mists the dropping water sounded like rain on the water surface.

If indeed the Marquess was willing to spend £300 on a dewpond, Thomas Davis, who had the entire Longleat estate under his direction, was less keen:

> The custom of making sheep ponds with rammed chalk is very expensive, many sheep ponds on the downs having cost from £25-40 and after all they are liable to be injured by every frosty winter and every dry summer and are very difficult to be repaired. A cheaper and more durable mode of making sheep ponds is much wanted in this district .... Much expense would be saved if care were taken to dig them on the highest points of the hills .... thus kept full by rain and fogs, and, by loose stones laid upon the rammed chalk are less liable to injury by the tread of sheep or cattle, as well as less subject to damage by heat or frost.

What and Who

During his years of research Martin heard of professional dewpond makers: "It is stated that there is at least one wandering gang of men who will construct for the modern farmer a dew pond .... which will contain more water in the heat of the summer than during the winter rains ...."

The Cruse family would not have felt flattered by his description. They had lived in Imber village, on Salisbury Plain, since the eighteenth century, and were proud of their skill. The work was seasonal, beginning annually on September 12th (except, presumably, when that day fell on the Sabbath) and they toured the countryside for six or seven months, weather being the decisive factor:

> They would be recommended to lodgings, and return to them year after year, for in those days the men of Imber were cleanly in person and character, upright, trusty and trustful, and they paid ready money for their simple needs. For their lodgings they paid 2/6 for five nights, for sleeping accommodation and their cooking. They provided their own food, and returned home for Saturday and Sunday.

Dew ponds could rarely be made during the summer. High on the downs, unshaded, weilding those heavy rammers, heaving the clay and rubble – men might have endured, but not their chalk and clay puddling. Labour costs would put summer work out of reach of most farmers. The Cruses provided a whole battery of their own tools, from wheelbarrows and digging implements to a spirit level pegged to a six-foot length of wood. The farmer provided carts and materials, and paid about £40, out of which the senior Mr Cruse paid wages, and for necessary repairs to the tools.

One of the earlier Cruses – John, in the early nineteenth century - owned a horse and cart, with which he took men and tools from site to site. It was no luxury; they travelled far afield to Kent, Berkshire, Hampshire, and Somerset as well as Wiltshire. A typical pond-making team worked in the late nineteenth century; Joel Cruse, in partnership with his brother-in-law Jabez Early, employed Daniel Pearce and Charles White as assistants at eighteen shillings weekly. They were less fortunate than John. The horse and cart had gone; everything was pushed on a barrow, even as far as Kent. John had supplemented the pond work by laying cottage floors in similar fashion – flint, chalk, and chopped straw. Jabez and Joel eked out a summer living in the harvest fields, but their great pride still lay in pond work; as Joel called it, "The making of a small reservoir or dew pond, so called because of its dependence on the natural fall of rain or dew".

He was, in his way, an educated man; articulate, and mathematically competent: "Although this man might be unable to proceed to the eleven times table in arithmetic, he could calculate with accuracy, after quiet thought and measurement, the cost of the undertaking, and an estimate would be forthcoming. The farmer would usually accept these calculations of a man who had received no more education after he was seven or eight years of age, except at night school".

Night school? Everything must be put to use, even spare time, when most people would have taken much-needed rest.

To the farmer, the cost of a dew pond was considerably more than the £40 fee; the Cruse team excavated the selected site to a depth of eight feet, and the farmer was responsible for the removal of discarded soil, and the provision of seventy cartloads of clay for puddling; plus enough lime for two coats, and a wagonload of straw. It was not work which could be hurried. Puddling began in the centre, working outwards, perhaps two yards on the first day but progressively less as they approached the perimeter, gradually working the sloping sides level with the field. Each day's work must be pounded until it was glossy, and thoroughly protected by straw before evening. No work could be done on frosty days, and one

View from an overgrown Dew Pond: piped water supply and winter shelter make it possible to graze cattle on land once fit only for sheep

careless blow with a seven-pound rammer could ruin a day's work. Two coats of lime covered the clay, each one beaten until the men could see their faces in it. A wagonload of straw covered it like a prickly eiderdown, held in place by a nine-inch layer of rough earth. A wooden fence kept out horses and cattle; no wonder the men took pride in their skill.

One pond in particular caught Joel's imagination. It crowned a hill near a Wiltshire village; so high a hill that the pond was on a level with the tip of the church spire. It is still there; still, there remains the stump of the hawthorn planted by the Cruse team to condense the mist and fog; still, water lies there, and a few remnants of the tough fence. The whole pond, perhaps thirty feet across, still a perfect circle; still within sight and sound of lambing pens; still within sight of dried-up dew ponds on a neighbouring hill.

Two other ponds remained in his memory for a different reason. They lay between Imber and Market Lavington; Shettle's pond, and Shore's pond, named after men who were said to have drowned themselves there, though a dew pond would seem rather shallow for the purpose. A mysterious tragedy was unearthed when the team commenced a dew pond on home ground. They dug on Chapel Down near Imber windmill, and found a mass grave. The cause was not identified – battle or plague – and the earth was replaced, and a pond made elsewhere.

Joel, in 1923, was in the last year of his life, viewing the decay of his little industry with an old man's disappointment: "due to the unwillingness of men to engage in work of so laborious a nature, and at a rate of payment which cannot be met by landowners or farmers".

This was not entirely so. There was, of course, the inevitable development of pumping systems by which water was easily taken to the top of any hill, or wherever else required. But a neighbouring village, Market Lavington, had had its own family of dew pond makers for at least two centuries. They claimed to have been in possession of a "secret process", though the secret seems to have been rather an open one. In 1915 Dr Williams Freeman published his Introduction to Field Archaeology, which received a glowing review in the Wiltshire Archaeological Magazine. He described the method of dew pond construction as followed in Lavington:

> First a layer of clay is carefully kneaded and beaten down with much force on the bare chalk. Over this is spread and carefully smoothed out a layer of freshly slaked lime three or four inches thick (to keep out the worms); on this is laid a layer of straw to protect the lime, and over all, six inches of chalk rubble to keep cattle from treading and breaking the clay puddling.

It seems paradoxical that whereas the hooves of cattle and horses could be useful instruments during primary puddling, once a pond was established, the laboriously created surface must be protected from them and from sheep by rubble. The Smiths of Market Lavington had to observe the same precautions as the Cruse family of Imber, secret process or no secret process.

Fifteen years after Joel's death, the Smiths were still in business, still claiming their secret process; one of their trade leaflets claimed that the firm, now working from Bedfordshire, could apply the process to the making of lakes, either high or low lying, and guaranteed to retain clear water without pumps. To Joel, a low-lying dew pond would have been a contradiction in terms. To apply the principle of condensation of dew or mist on a low site, in the expectation of creating a lake "whereby the pleasures of wild duck shooting, fishing, boating, swimming etc can be enjoyed" - it would need to be a very powerful secret. Not only that, but the Smiths had diversified tremendously; water divining, well sinking. pumping plant installed – anything connected with water. They attracted a certain amount of attention. In those days, with television still in its infancy, radio had its own chat show; In Town Tonight. One of the Smiths was featured in November, 1937, but by no means exclusively as a dew pond maker.

What, and When

There was a consensus of opinion; Thomas Davis, Gilbert White, Edward Martin, the Cruse family, working shepherds - all agreed that the only suitable place for a dew pond was the top of a high hill.

Men of the Bronze Age located their hill forts similarly; from those high ramparts they could keep constant watch against attack.

When it came, flocks, herds and tribe were gathered to that safe eminence; food was comparatively simple to provide – what of water?

Necessity, coupled with their innate ingenuity, would in all probability have suggested dew ponds. Those natural depressions on the chalk heights, with or without a residual layer of clay, lying in the path of so many large hooves, must at some time have held water. Men of such intelligence would work out the rest according to their own need. If any historical hypothesis may be presumed accurate, it is this. No one could seriously claim that visible signs of such ancient dew ponds remain after so many thousands of years, but reason affirms their use.

Old Dew Ponds make convenient sites for bonfires and rubbish

The most ancient pond known to the writer is on Milk Hill, behind the White Horse of Alton Barnes. The Saxons made a survey of the district in 825 A.D. and the name by which they referred to that pond is significant. Remembering the Sussex farm worker who drove his team of oxen round and round the chalk bed of a damaged dew pond, effecting its repair, surely it is possible that the broad hooves of oxen were similarly used in Saxon times. No opportune salvation in time of need, as in the Bronze Age; rather, an established method of creating a useful reservoir. No complications with straw, or successive layers of clay; simply the heavy animals, trampling the damp chalk until it bonded, glossy and waterproof.

The name? Oxen Mere.

The natural historian, H.W.Timperley, explored the ancient high track from Liddington to Ramsbury. It is unusual among downland tracks in being shaded by bushes and trees. That layer of clay found in dew pond depressions had, along this ridge, settled deeply enough to foster even the growth of oak trees. It gave the double advantage of natural screening from which there was a high, clear view of the surrounding country for many miles:

> After days spent on open downland tracks, long stretches of which were only picked out by the greener turf .... as they wound to and for over sky-touching crests, it was strange to be shut in like that in the same countryside. Nothing that could be seen from the lane gave clearer indications of its position than the dew ponds spaced out along it – in this the lane was like any other old trackway on the downs. There are no springs at these altitudes on the chalk. One obviously artificial depression just inside a coppice of oak and hazel had been, if I am not mistaken, an old dew pond; it had an oak growing in the bottom of the cup, a tree no younger than those in the hedges and most of those in the wood. Dew ponds are not made under trees, and where there are dew ponds or the remains of dew ponds along an old road today it is more than likely that they replaced earlier ones and these replaced others earlier still, giving a continuous succession from the unrecorded times when these ridgeways from earthwork to earthwork were more trodden by men and their flocks than they are today.

.... and Where

Most dew ponds have fallen into disuse; the problem of water supply has been simplified beyond recognition by the use of power, and only circular grass-covered depressions remain on the hills as reminders of bygone times. There is little general knowledge of their whereabouts.

However, we do have information about the many ponds functioning two centuries ago. Adams and Dury's map showed, not only a white horse with perky ears, but a host of dew ponds. The map was sponsored by the nobility and gentry of the county, and all their residences were shown. Cottages, in which shepherds might have lived, do not appear; but sheep ponds are meticulously marked, emphasising the fact that the county was heavily dependent upon that industry. Some of the great houses and gracious residences would not have existed without it.

The ponds along the Liddington-Ramsbury Ridge, recorded by Timperley in the third decade of this century, are not on the map, but a hundred and fifty years lay between its publication and Joel Cruse's realisation that his family industry had died; plenty of time for several generations of pond makers to build a succession of small oases as they were needed.

That fascinating map also includes a red herring. Browsing happily, one moves south of Devizes, and on the eastern spur of Fuzz Hill, almost blurred into the drawing of its steep slope, is the legend "Drew's Pond". Momentarily one is tempted to suspect a misprint, but it seems like rank disrespect where Adams and Dury are concerned, and of course dew pond was not the term then in use. In fact the pond in question was a very large one, belonging to Drew's water mill. The Drew family had owned it since the early seventeenth century, and Adams and Dury were, as ever, correct.

Footnote

Dew ponds provided drink for sheep and other animals; they also refreshed wild birds, but they did so without benefit of dew. They were sustained by rain, augmented by condensed mist or fog.

During winter, in the valleys, sheep were sometimes hay-fed, and very thirsty; Joel Cruse remarked upon the amount of water a thirsty sheep could consume - as much as two gallons, though root

Suspected Dew Pond near West Kennet

crops contained more moisture, reducing the thirst a little. Even so, had their diet been so dehydrating when on the downs, no dew pond could have survived the onslaught of even a small flock.

The downland diet was, of course, pasture: grass, laden morning and evening with dew.

Whether it had descended from above, or ascended from beneath, it was, on those chalk hills, a main constituent of the animals' moisture intake, except during periods of severe drought. Grass-fed sheep were dew-fed sheep, no matter what was in the dew pond.

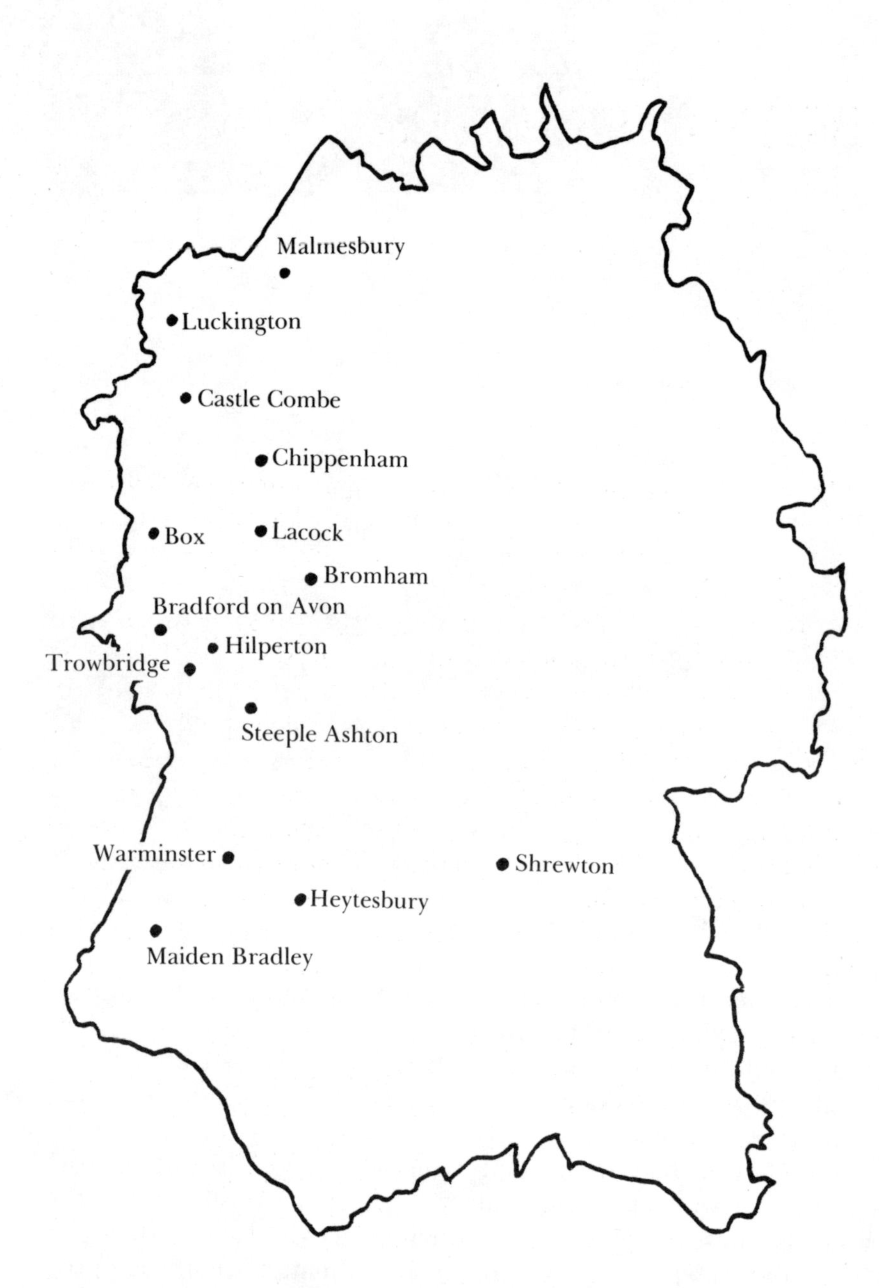

BLIND HOUSES

BLIND HOUSES

These miniature prison houses were a refinement of torture for the claustrophobic. Usually stone-built, some had scarcely enough room for one person to stretch, yet they frequently had to accommodate several suspects at a time; innocent and guilty, drunkard and starving, clean and otherwise - all in together. The only reasons for separation were difference of sex, or difference of opinion. Brawlers sometimes needed a guard to keep them apart.

Windows were always lacking; hence the name, blind house. The only light and ventilation came from tiny grilles, high in the walls. When the walls were of thick stone, the efficiency of the grilles was materially reduced. Negligible light and less air; the only thing to guide prisoners to the earth closet in the corner was the smell. For a resting place there might be straw, or an iron cradle fixed to the wall; otherwise, the stone floor. Any daytime warmth was kept out by the thickness of the walls; damp, dark and chill – they were nearly all the same, and any sign of protest was met by chaining the culprit to iron staples in the wall.

Many blind houses were free-standing, built of stone blocks, with heavy nail-studded wooden doors which look as forbidding as the rest of the structure, though legend has it that they provided comfort. Where the door has an outsize keyhole, there is usually a local story of a prisoner being refreshed by friends; a pint pot, with the bowl of a churchwarden pipe (scrubbed, perchance) immersed in the ale, and the stem poked through the keyhole. Other doors have a couple of inches of space underneath. There, saucers of tea have been supplied. The spirit of the Red Cross parcel is older than one might suppose.

Blind house shapes vary. Square, round, rectangular, octagonal; sometimes to suit the site and space available, sometimes apparently to suit the builder's whim. Names also vary. In Wiltshire, blind house is generally used, but other names include round house, lock-up, clink (uncomfortably evocative) cage or bund house. They vary according to the county. Sufkep is a rarity from further north, shortened from safe-keep.

England has over a hundred and there are more in Wales. Officially Scotland has none. Tolbooths served the same purpose, but there might be forgotten specimens in isolated places. Local guardians of the peace – in rural England, the parish constable – needed a secure place in which to put drunks, rowdies, tramps, disreputable women, two halves of a fight - the superfluous folk about whom society did not wish to know. Blind houses were also needed whilst awaiting transport to take those accused of greater offences to county gaols to await trial. For very minor offenders just the rattle of the keys was enough.

This is not fully understood unless one has been inside such a prison. There is one at Lacock; a potent deterrent. One step over the threshold brings the penetrating chill around and within; slow, sinister and lonely. The iron staples to which prisoners were chained are still there. The original door lies against the thick stone wall; with that in place, heavily reinforced with iron, isolation would be complete. Neither would the prospect of company be encouraging.

Wiltshire Blind Houses

Most date from the eighteenth century; some, from the early nineteenth century; two of the known Wiltshire specimens are earlier. One of these is more in the nature of a tolbooth. Chippenham has a "Yelde Hall" built in the fifteenth century, within which is the old lock-up, at the bottom of stone steps from the main hall. Unusually, the ceiling is only timber; however, pondering the tough timbers of tithe barns which bid fair to complete a thousand years in situ, perhaps one should rescind the word "only"

Lacock Blind House adjacent to the Tithe Barn

The other Wiltshire blind house in which wood was used, is Bromham. There, the rectangular prison is based on brick, and built into the churchyard wall, but its walls and door are timber under a stone-tiled roof. In later years, no longer required for punishment, it was used as a coal store, as were many such buildings; they held coal, oil, or paint and building materials. At Maiden Bradley, the old blind house belongs to a restaurant; it has

Maiden Bradley Blind House

been thoroughly cleaned, re-lined and whitewashed. Small windows admit more light, and cans and bottles of soft drinks are stored in neat racks. The usual blind house chill prevails because of the thickness of the walls, but now it is in a good cause, chilling drinks rather than hearts and hopes. Vive la Difference!

Box blind house is square. Whereas most free-standing specimens have a rustic appearance - perhaps put up by the little man round the corner - this has elegance, as if it was once on the drawing board, destined to be a mausoleum. Yet here it is, out on the street; just one more blind house, and obviously needed. The step is well worn.

Castle Combe has one, but built at the rear of a cottage – a tough stone lean-to in which a prisoner of large girth would feel severely restricted. Like Maiden Bradley it is now in domestic use.

Heytesbury and Hilperton are both set into garden walls. Backs to the wall, as it were, but facing the road. Heytesbury is much the worse for wear, though it still has the original heavily-nailed door with the old padlock. Hilperton has been renovated. Apart from the replica door, it has the domed roof with a boss finial which is the most common type in Wiltshire. So has Shrewton, a neatly rounded little lock-up; almost a pleasure to be in clink when it has so dapper an appearance, but doubtless the uniform inner chill would dispel any such nonsense. Some years ago, road widening necessitated a small adjustment. The blind house was dismantled, and its stones were numbered and rebuilt a few yards away to avoid obstruction.

Luckington is a thoroughly blind house; no grills, no gaping keyhole - just an iron flap. A visitor can feel the chill even though the door is closed.

Steeple Ashton was a village with careful officials. They built their blind house and kept the bill: £19.18s in 1773 – a goodly sum, but William Rawlins made a goodly job of it. A blind house needed foundations no less than any other house:

> diging foundation of Building and ruff work to rise ground high .... to paving inside of house ....

All good thick stone, topped with a dome and boss, and with the resultant inner chill. Legend states that the last prisoner, about the turn of the last century, died of pneumonia during the night. Not so. He died after having been taken out at the end of his night's stay, though it was small comfort to him, or to the constable who never again used William Rawlins' handiwork.

Warminster blind house has no chill, no whisper of past miseries. It has rubble walls which from one angle look square. Walk a little further and the square becomes a rectangle; walk the other way and the blind house melts into the wall of the adjacent garage. Free of old restraints, it is ready and willing to play jokes – an impression aided and abetted by the tiled, rounded roof with a flattened boss, just like a cheeky beret. Inside, the building is used as a garden shed with all the familiar tools and the fresh smell of earth. The inner walls are smoke-stained; before the gardening days, bacon was cured here. This small house recovered from its blindness long since.

Little recognisable trace remains of Amesbury blind house. Occupants have changed often , and they have altered the building to suit their own requirements; now, there is nothing except two blocks fixed to the floor. The two original cells had one block each, to which prisoners were chained. Now, those blocks are strangely surrounded by an estate agent's impedimenta, with lavish information about mod cons within desirable residences.

Steeple Ashton Blind House at the centre of the village

Trowbridge, the largest and outwardly the sturdiest of the dome-and-finial type, was supposedly secure; but little can withstand pent-up desperation bred through decades of slow hunger. The story of the great riot of 1826 has often been told; strangers pause beside the blind house plaque, and wonder how unarmed rioters could tear such a roof from those massive walls. Less often mentioned is the fact that there were other similar riots. As far back as 1738, long before Napoleon set Europe ablaze, weavers were distraught rather than distressed. Rumours that a local cloth merchant had lowered his prices brought a mob - weavers, shearmen and boys - gathered from Trowbridge and Bradford and all the outlying villages. They broke into the workshop and cut all the loom chains. Conciliation was tried; the merchant promised to pay them another penny a yard, but they pressed on, broke into his house and wrecked it. Clothing, curtains, bedclothes, feather beds, furniture; all shredded, smashed, and thrown into the river. Back in the market place they demanded - and got – a written guarantee on a minimum price. All but one went home; he was found looting the ruined house, and was arrested. The rest sent an order to the Justices to release him; when this was refused, nine more houses belonging to the merchant, together with his grist and fulling mills, were wrecked.

Ninety years passed, in which hunger had not eased, and the terror of destitution had grown. To the descendants of the men who had torn chains from looms and wrecked machinery, Trowbridge blind house was no great obstacle.

Malmesbury, as far as blind houses go, is unique. It has two. At first sight. they are a pair. No domes, no finials. From the market place the Abbey grounds are entered through an arched gateway with two gatehouses, one each side. Each is a blind house, but they are not alike. On the right there is maximum security. The heavy door has two large keyholes, one covered by an iron hasp; the hinges are hefty enough to last a millennium. The stone beside the keyholes has been scratched away from the inside by some desperate captive; there is neither light nor ventilation, and the door is heavily studded.

To the left, the gatehouse provided a more indulgent prison. The sole keyhole has no iron cover; there is even a simple thumb latch needing no key at all; studding on the door is sparse.

Box Blind House

Bradford on Avon blind house has everything. Unusual position, unusual history; its age is both unusual and uncertain. Like Trowbridge, it has two cells to separate potential pugilists and male from female.

It has been claimed that there is a second blind house in the town; a tiny room above the chamber in which the justices once sat in Belcombe House. However, this would have been a mere waiting room during the hearing; hardly a blind house as usually understood.

The old town bridge spanned the Avon for four centuries, and it had a chapel. This was customary, for travellers needed the prayers of a holy man, and alms must be collected for the upkeep of the bridge and road. At Bradford they were also necessary for the nearby leper hospital of St Margaret. That chapel was an integral part of the bridge, which by the late sixteenth century needed extensive repair. As soon as possible, early in the next century, bridge and chapel were repaired, but no one knows precisely what work was done on the chapel. It was still perched on the cutwater at the end of the medieval arches, its front an integral part of the parapet. Aubrey noticed it in his travels: "Here is a strong and handsome bridge in the middest of which there is a little chapel ...."

The lovingly crafted finial is surmounted by a copper gudgeon, a fish being one of the Christian symbols, and a suitable choice for a chapel in such a location.

Its metamorphosis from chapel to blind house possibly coincided with the eruption of industrial violence in the early eighteenth century, but there is no certain record of the event. The leper hospital had disappeared at the Dissolution, and roads needed more than alms to pay for their upkeep, therefore any changes involved only the use of the building. At some time a chimney was added, but no fireplace; again, a partition was built to separate the sexes, or the quarrelsome. The chimney was in place before 1808, when John Buckler painted a watercolour of the Town Bridge, including the blind house and its chimney. The partition was not yet in place by 1833, when the accounts include the following items:

3 day keep for E. Box 1s6d
3 day keep for Love 1s6d
Guard to keep Box and Love apart 2s6d

The blind house is square, built of stone blocks, with the original oak door plentifully studded with large nails. It has more light and air than most, the grilles being less inaccessible, and also able to catch any breeze from the river.

In 1757 William Hitchens, a follower of John Wesley, was taken in Bradford by the press gang. Afterwards, he wrote a letter:

> Reverend and Dear Sir,
> .... at Bradford I was pressed for a soldier, and carried to an inn where the gentlemen were. Mr Pearse came and offered bail .... they said they would take his word, but not for me; I must go to the little round house, the stone room on the side of the bridge .... There I found nothing to sit on but a stone .... soon after a friend sent me a chair on which I sat all night. I had a double guard, twelve soldiers in all .... my soul was at liberty; even there I found some work to do for God; I had a fair opportunity of speaking to them who durst not leave me, and I hope it was not in vain .... in the afternoon I was carried before the Commissioners, and part of the Act was read which empowered them to take such ablebodied men as followed no business .... Then I said "If these are the men you are to take, I am not a proper person, for I do have a lawful calling in partnership with my brother".

After considerable argument he was allowed bail, and hurried away to Cornwall for James, his brother, to support him, and to find written evidence of his work and property. He wrote the whole story to John Wesley: "I hope you will return God thanks for my deliverance out of the hands of unreasonable and wicked men".

Constables

These were absolutely in the amateur tradition; usually a mixed array of tradesmen – butcher, yeoman, plumber, clerk, brewer, printer, clothier (cloth manufacturer), cordwainer, plasterer, carpenter, and a few gentlemen. The reasoning behind that list was that tradesmen had common sense. Intelligent enough to keep their own accounts and run their own businesses, they could run the blind house in a suitable manner, organise necessary cleaning and repair, arrage for the transport of the inmates when necessary, and keep honest accounts. The few gentlemen were appointed less for those services than to act as advisers; when in trouble, ask the gentry. Only rarely did they fail.

Though there was a certain pride in having such authority, it was also an irritant. A busy tradesman with his way to make and a family to keep could ill afford the time needed for the work of a constable; it was not always troublesome, but if a serious crime occurred, he could be back and forth from one week's end to another. It was a busy period when Benjamin Taylor of Chippenham held office, in 1822:

	£	s	d
In charge of the Prisoners			
12 days and nights	1.	10.	0
In the following September:			
To Horse and Caravan and myself			
to Devizes taking Prsioners (sic)		14.	0
To turnpikes		2.	1

There was an official guide to these charges, according to a sad little note on the back of an account for £7.7s.:

> Allowed only half the within bill being £3.13.6d not having read the county Allowance.

William Spencer's arithmetic left him short:

	£	s	d
Expenses for Horse and Self	0.	12.	6
Horse and Self one day		6.	0
11 days and nights as Special Constable in			
charge of the Prisoners and taking them	1.	7.	6
	2.	5.	0

Bradford on Avon Blind House: a unique site

It was better when Mr Figgins saw to the finances:

> Rec'd Nov.4th 1822 of Mr Figgins Churchwarden the sum of one pound 7/6 for 11 days and nights over prisoners as Special Constable. Wm Spencer.

Mr Figgins needed plenty of petty cash when James Moore went to Salisbury to escort necessary witnesses:

> 9/- beer, 5/- spirits, 1/6 beer for coachman and postboys, 6/- beer on return of witness.

Mr Figgins paid.

It was not all escort duty. A Bradford constable incurred £1.15s in expances (sic) attending the discovery of C.Hanny's first wife. Also at Bradford the constable submitted an account after having tended a dying man; perhaps one of the unfortunate vagrants who so often occupied the blind houses. This one was more kindly treated than most; the items include gin and tobacco - one hopes that some at least went to the patient. Then came a claim for 2s3d for Burying a Donkey (no gin) by order of Esq. Tugwell. But the constable who led the field in going over and above the call of duty submitted his account in May 1823:

> Constable for going and Apprehending and marrying John Eastman 10s0d

The 1830s were frantic times for constables. Farm workers protested against the new machinery; weavers were crazed by fear and hunger, and the blind houses were never empty. Constables and churchwardens were constantly ordering cleaners for the privy, the straw, and the whitewashing; they needed the smith to mend the handcuffs (broke by Dunny,) two men to guard the blind house, another for attendance on the stocks; there was a constant succession of prisoners to admit or release; then there were six men inside, all at once, and to add to their difficulties Sarah had to go also:

> Bed and guard for Sarah.
> 6 men in Blind House 3s6d

One particular fact strikes the reader of these accounts. The constables and churchwardens kept detailed records, some more easily than others, for reading, writing and cyphering were not general accomplishments. They were short of time; they must often have been anxious about their own neglected affairs. Occasionally they must have been sorely tried.

Yet, though blind house prisoners all had to be entered in those detailed accounts, if they were eventually acquitted, the reason for their arrest was carefully omitted from the records. Also, people who might reasonably be suspect, and therefore put into the blind house, sometimes had a pleasant surpise:

Box Parish. May 3rd 1767
Paid: Edward Salter 1s0d
(to be off)

Hilperton Blind House shaken by heavy traffic

The Magistrates

Magistrates sat in judgement, but in many cases they knew the accused and took a compassionate view. Thus, in 1707 Thomas Daniel Ody was brought from Pewsey blind house, to appear before a man with a famous name; Edward Seymour:

> .... convicted before Ed. Seymour Esqre for cutting and stealing ye wood of Farmer Pye for which he was sentenced to pay two shillings to ye poore of ye Parish .... This being ye first offence.

This may not seem very impressive, until one reads the Salisbury assize lists, in which Richard Waite was sentenced to death for maliciously cutting down trees. He was reprieved, but the punishment was available if the magistrate thought fit.

Waite was tried by Mr Justice Burrough. Twenty-one men were brought to Salisbury Assizes that day, in 1723, from the surrounding countryside - probably via caravan from their blind houses - and they were all on capital charges; ten for burglary, four for stealing from the person, two for housebreaking, one for theft above the value of 40s from a house, two for horse stealing, and one for sheep stealing, together with Richard Waite. All were convicted on the evidence; all were sentenced to death according to law. And all twenty-one were reprieved.

Even so, constables did not always feel that the Bench was against them, making nothing of their efforts. In 1822 a Justice of the Peace put in a strong report in the constables' favour:

> .... and I further certify that the usual allowances made on such occasions are wholly inadequate and insufficient ....

There is a touching account of a case in which the Justice of the Peace, in his compassion, seems to have accepted diminishing returns - indeed I would go so far as to say he engineered them:

> October 15th 1745
>
> Be it remembered that William Dowden of the parish of Little Chiverel in the county of Wilts on August 9th was convicted before me at the complaint of John Wadman of

Imber Esq for carrying a gun and shooting of pigeons for which I made an order upon him for payment of £2.10s for the use of the poor where the offence was committed. The informer gave William Dowden the money forfeited to him. By the intercession of friends, considering him as a poor man, I gave him back £1.15s. The rest to Richard Godwin 5s to John Perrat's wife 5s. To my clerk for his trouble and expenses 5s.

One strongly suspects that William Dowden was reimbursed for those last three payments before he parted company with that J.P. (Mr Hunt) and the forgiving John Wadman.

Benevolent or otherwise, magistrates must at times have been subject to acute dyspepsia. Riots were all too frequent in mid-eighteenth century; however courageously the constables faced the rioters and put them in the blind houses, and transported them to Salisbury Assizes; however impartial or compassionate a magistrate tried to be, the jury could bring it all to nothing; a waste of time for constables and magistrates. Eighteen rioters were brought for trial:

1) Isaac Coles, after full and clear evidence that he was one of the leaders in cutting down a turnpike, acquitted by the jury. 2) Wm Denmeades, another principal, tried by a new jury. Acquitted. King's Counsel found it useless to try any more. 3) Wm Davis, very old and deaf, discharged. Other eleven bound over to appear at next assizes at Taunton. No bills found against the others.

There were no doubts, no room for leniency, in the Hilperton murder trial. Daniel Bayley was murdered on November 20th 1828. He had been to the Lion and Fiddle as usual, then set off for home. After a few minutes Moses Angel and Richard Mizen were seen to follow him. Some time later another customer, walking home across the fields, found Bayley unconscious and bleeding profusely. He was carried back to the Lion and Fiddle and a doctor summoned. Then he was taken back home. He never regained consciousness, but it took him another four weeks to die.

Angel and Mizen went, via the blind house, to Salisbury for trial. Mizen was acquitted, though he had been with Angel that evening;

Bromham Blind House: wood under a stone roof

he seems to have been fortunate. Angel had sold Bayley's watch. His first reason was that he needed food and drink. When another prospective purchaser asked him about it, he said that it was his property, but his father had just bought him another for £4. He was hanged on the Saturday following the trial.

Lodging in stables was not permitted, even though there was no room anywhere else - except of course in the blind house. Edward Horlock Mortimer Esquire, J.P., dealt with Triphina White of the parish of Bradford on Avon. She was brought before him as a Singlewoman, A Rogue and a vagabond; on the 12th day of August 1821 she did (with others) wander abroad and lodge in a Stable in the Parish of Bradford and was apprehended by Robert Price, Constable. The Constable's reward was five shillings. Triphina's keep for one day in the blind house cost sixpence.

Warminster Blind House partially absorbed but still easily recognisable

Churchwardens

Ordinary men had every incentive to avoid the office of Constable. It not only took time which they needed for their own business, but it was impossible to please everyone in the parish; almost inevitably they would attract animosity. Therefore the churchwarden was, very occasionally, left holding a very difficult baby. At Shrewton he valiantly recorded the expenses incurred when going to the justices' meetings in Salisbury, but never itemised the bills for any of the journeys. Nemesis arrived in the shape of quarter day, and he settled to some massive arithmetic. There was a startling entry:

> Jan. 1813.
> Brought forward from behind £507.2s5¾d

> His medicine was better than his mathematics.

> October 1st. Gave Willis a treat for stones. 3s0d

Which may sound surprising until "treat" is replaced by the word he meant to use – treatment.

Other entries sound familiar, from the Bradford wardens:

> Keep for three boys for staling (sic) apples. 1s6d
> Keep for Batchlor comited for Exposeing his person 1s0d

Some churchwardens were uppish. Benjamin Banks, Constable, submitted his expense account early in September. His writing was rough but clear. The account is detailed; horse-hire, turnpikes, board for fifteen days - £7.10.6½d. He received nothing until November, then a receipt was written in meticulous copperplate:

> Received of John Figgins Churchwarden Esquire the sum of £7.10.6d being my full demand for Time, Board, and Expenses Attending on the Magistrates at Chippenham and Escorting the prisoners to Devizes and Salisbury Goals (sic). Benjamin Banks.

Even his signature was written for him. It was a pity about the discount. A halfpenny was worth having, but perhaps not at the price of a discussion with John Figgins Churchwarden Esquire.

Stocks and Pillory

Frequently, these were near the blind house, being also part of the customary shock treatment, which though sharp was rarely short; or so it seemed to the prisoners. In the stocks, they sat; legs straight out before them so that the feet were held by the ankles in the wooden clamp. In the pillory, they stood; usually on a platform, against a post with a wooden clamp at the top in which wrists and neck were held. Supervision was necessary, not only to prevent escape, but to restrain onlookers. They were allowed to throw rubbish – it was part of the punishment – but hard substances were forbidden. Usually it was fairly easy to check, but one person with a grudge plus Test Match delivery managed to make a cabbage stalk penetrate a prisoner's cheek.

Less attention may have been paid to the regulars. At Pewsey in 1707 the stocks were put to use.

> Arthur Cook of ye Parish of Pewsey was convicted of drunkenness by John Smith Esquire upon his own confession for which he got in ye stocks five hours according to ye statute in ye case provided.

A constable could earn from one shilling upwards according to the length of sentence prescribed, for supervision duties. At five hours, one assumes that Cook was a regular customer.

During the reign of Elizabeth Tudor, a prisoner was put in the pillory. He stood, hands and head clamped in place, and the pelting began. Inevitably he writhed and his feet moved on the wooden platform. It was rotten, and splintered beneath him so that he was left suspended by throat and wrists. The constable rescued him in time, but the case was not closed. The prisoner brought an action against the local authorities and was awarded damages.

In an age of swiftly-travelling news, this might have set a precedent, and the history of crime and punishment, at least in the case of petty offences, materially altered. It remained hidden; one scrap of paper among many others.

Shrewton Blind House

A Fate Worse than the Blind House?

Blind houses were never intended for long-term imprisonment; they provided short-term punishment or a break in the journey to a county jail. The chill and the darkness were frightening; the smell and suffocation when on occasion they were crowded, had caused sickness and even death. Was there anything worse?

As early as 1672, prisoners at Fisherton, Wiltshire's county jail, were complaining bitterly, and they were given a hearing at the Summer Assizes. Debtors were the main sufferers. The jailer, John Thorpe, prohibited the use of the courtyard during the day. He charged heavily for the use of the common room; for the privilege of sleeping on its bare floor, he charged two shillings per week. Visitors were either prohibited, or at best kept waiting for two or three hours when they brought food. In the prison rooms he had blocked the hearths so that fires were impossible even in the depth of winter. The window was blocked, through which food had always been passed:

> And by many other practices contrived subtily to distresse ye poore petitioners whose estates are consumed and health impaired so that for want of ayer (air) and necessaries they must perish unless relieved by yr Lordships ....

Nothing else was recorded at the time; if any relief was given, it was temporary. A century later, two prisoners were allowed to stand outside the jail, each one padlocked by the leg to a chain fixed to a wall. There they stood all day, trying to persuade passers-by to buy small articles made by the prisoners; nets, laces and purses. At Christmas, selected prisoners were permitted to go through the town, chained together, carrying a sack and begging for extra food and money. Surely the blind house was preferable. By 1784 the Justices had appointed a salaried jailer. He was forbidden to trade with the prisoners, or charge them. No drink could be sold inside the prison or brought in. Visitors were permitted by order of the justices, and there were now single cells; twenty-four of them.

It sounds as though things had improved, but one man, when sentenced to a year's imprisonment there, pleaded to be hanged instead. Which is, indeed, food for thought.

Trowbridge Blind House: the largest

Were Blind Houses a Deterrent?

For poor creatures like Triphina White they were unavoidable. A vagabond because she had no home; homeless because no one would offer shelter to a vagabond. A Singlewoman (sic) and a Rogue; it seems that she was also plain, perhaps ugly. A woman with any physical attraction would have been arrested as a prostitute, given that her other circumstances were similar. Triphina was caught in the trap of homelessness, dirt, hunger, and nights in the blind house. It was no deterrent; just a regular part of her life.

Cook, the drunkard, at least enjoyed oblivion during his drunken spells; periods in the stocks or blind house, even though they tended to get longer, were a fair price to pay; he probably took it all for granted.

In Steeple Ashton towards the end of 1830 it seemed that the blind house built with such care was less of a deterrent than they had hoped. There was a spirit of hate abroad; an arsonist, firing their stacks and even their houses while they slept. Nothing had been seen until the flames leapt high; nothing found, to connect the activity with any known miscreant. The Constable did his best, but one man working alone was usually the length of the village away from the next fire. It was a time of fear.

On November 29th there was a village meeting. They arranged a rota; every night for the next two weeks there would be a watch from four in the afternoon, at dusk, until seven next morning. In each watch there would be five men; one of the principal farmers as leader, with four other men acting as special constables. The latter would receive 2s per duty, to be paid by the farmer in charge before they dispersed.

The next meeting was arranged for December 13th at eleven o'clock; at the Coach and Horses. Were they expecting to celebrate an arrest? A canny fire-raiser would have waited, striking again on the 14th, but there was no further mention of the matter. With so many opponents, the odds on being thrust into that blind house were much greater. Perhaps it had been worth the expense after all.

Lost Blind Houses

In 1902 an official list of blind houses was made. It omitted those at Bromham, Warminster and Castle Combe. By 1924, predictably, the official number was lower; eleven. Such unimportant little buildings had been neglected during the intervening years. During the Edwardian era the rich lived joyously and the poor lived anxiously; during the terrible years of the Great War everyone had other things to think about. Such small buildings were of no concern; their historical value was unrecognised, and many crumbled.

By 1978 the official number had again changed. Maiden Bradley, Malmesbury and Amesbury had supposedly disappeared; also Colerne, Downton, Pewsey and Sutton Benger. Castle Combe had been missed entirely. The Mann family had built a mausoleum in Trowbridge Cemetery which looks very much like a blind house, except that it is more spacious. Authentic blind houses, other than the free-standing type, are easily incorporated into other buildings, so that their original purpose is forgotten.

Amesbury is a prime example. Its corner site made it attractive to shopkeepers; the wide curved front has been a shop window for a florist, a motor cycle shop, a milk bar, and now an estate agent. The only remaining indications of its origin are those two blocks in the floor.

Southwick blind house stood in its battered state at the side of the main road until the Queen's Silver Jubilee. Then, it was demolished. In its place, there is a small garden with seats for passers-by, and a plaque to preserve the memory of other days; a very pleasing notion.

Melksham lock-up, on no official list, stood in the middle of the market place. There is still a faded sepia photograph in the museum at Devizes. So many road signs sprouted from its dome that it seems to be wearing a Red Indian bonnet. An amusing specimen, but long ago demolished and almost completely forgotten.

Pewsey also had one in its market place; Arthur Cook might have known it. Colerne's was in the main village street, and the Downton example stood near the workhouse, where a factory now stands. I have found no mention of these in any of the parish records; which remark may well be the signal for the re-appearance of forgotten references by the score.

The blind houses which remain exist in a society which has recently developed a great awareness and appreciation of local history. They, and the records of everything concerning them, are now certain of preservation, and of their place in that branch of history which tells of ordinary people. We owe as much to them as to the great ones whose names fill the indices of the history books, and it is hoped that people who now glance occasionally at blind houses will do so with understanding.

George Bernard Shaw, in his wisdom, expressed it well:

> "Imprisonment cannot be fully understood by those who do not understand freedom."

Existing Blind Houses

Box	On A4 at south end of village
Bradford on Avon	Town Bridge
Bromham	Corner of churchyard
Castle Combe	Behind cottage next to Inn. Not accessible.
Chippenham	Inside Yelde Hall. Preliminary enquiry by phone.
Heytesbury	A36 middle if village on left going to Salisbury
Hilperton	A361 opposite The Knap beside War Memorial
Lacock	East Street at end of Tithe Barn
Luckington	B4040 Bristol Road
Maiden Bradley	Annexe at end of Locksmith's Restaurant on village green
Malmesbury	Abbey gateway by Market Cross
Shrewton	A344 beside road in village
Steeple Ashton	Village Green
Trowbridge	Town Bridge
Warminster	In garage yard by The Obelisk at end of Church Street
Amesbury	Ought possibly to be listed among the "lost" blind houses as nothing but the blocks remain.

A grim detail of Steeple Ashton Blind House

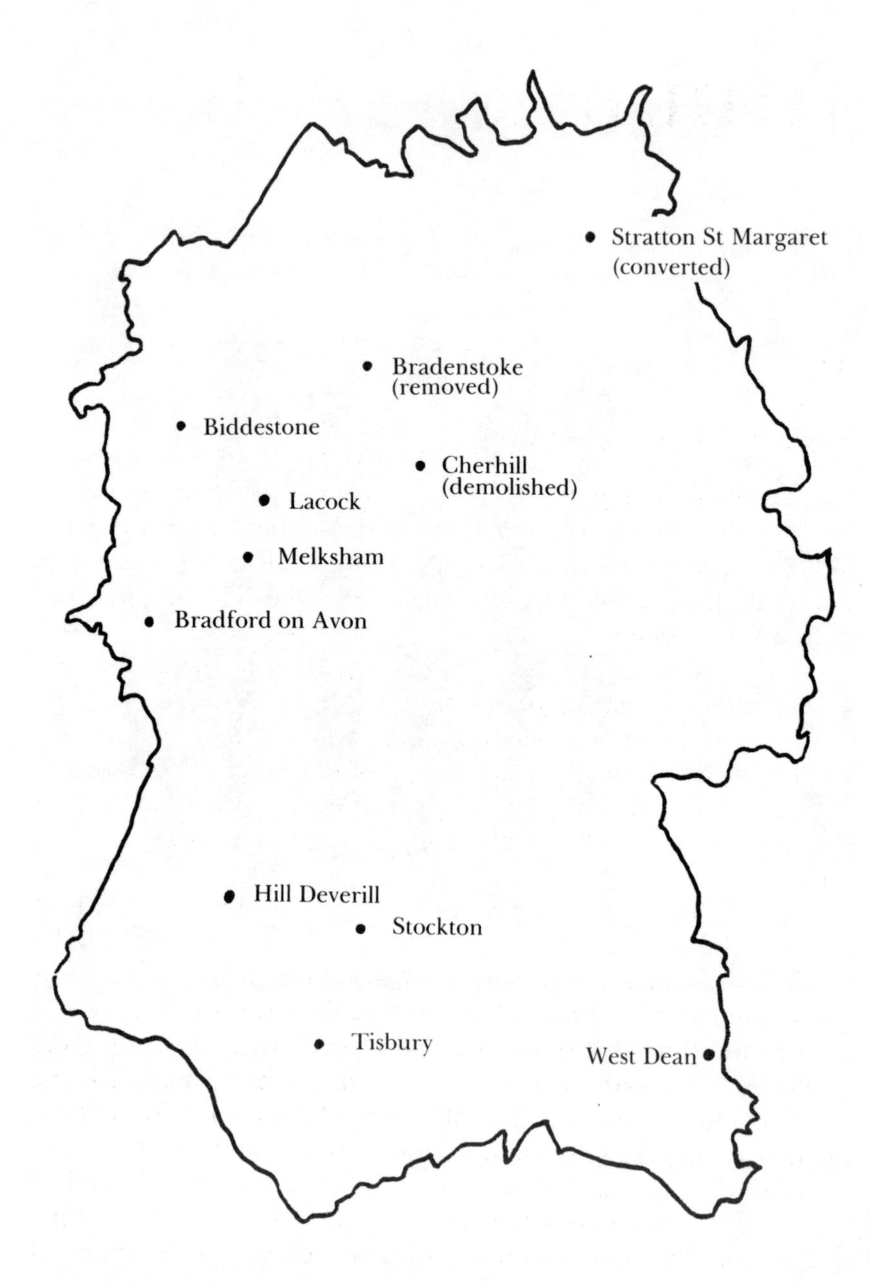
Stratton St Margaret
(converted)
Bradenstoke
(removed)
Biddestone
Cherhill
(demolished)
Lacock
Melksham
Bradford on Avon
Hill Deverill
Stockton
Tisbury
West Dean

TITHE BARNS

TITHE BARNS

When is a tithe barn not a tithe barn? – when it was built for use as a farm building. There is a general impression that large barns were all tithe barns, and that tithe barns were all purpose-built in medieval times to hold vast taxes paid in kind to abbeys and other church foundations.

Yet a great barn was just as necessary to a wealthy landowning layman as to a monastic community; both had to store crops from home farms; tools and produce must be protected, and tenants often paid their rent in kind, necessitating more storage space. Abbots' corn or any other corn – all must be threshed, and the best place for that was between the high, draughty doorways of a big barn.

What of the tithe? The proportion was constant; one tenth of arable and animal produce and all other earnings. Naturally the total varied according to circumstances. Where the population was sparse their total was less. One tenth of the produce of poor soil must be less than that from richer ground. The tenth sucking pig would be less meaty in some districts than others, though if the owner could so contrive, it would always be the runt. Some tithe barns were surprisingly small; the most surprising thing about any, whatever their size, is that they survived at all. The imposition they represented was so hated that many must have been destroyed time and again. The tithe lasted a thousand years; a millennium of resentment, which began with murder.

Tithes Great and Little

Offa, King of Mercia, ruled for forty years until almost the end of the eighth century. His realm extended from the Humber to the Severn, and eventually over most of the Home Counties. To rule so great an area in those days needed daring, a limited conscience, connections in higher places, and money.

Much of his money came from the wool trade. Wool, from the sheep which thronged the downs and valleys; woven into a uniquely heavy cloth, much of it was made into voluminous ankle-length cloaks for the export trade. Wind and weather-proof, one cloak would cover a man and his mount; wrapped several times around the man, it served as bed and blankets. Charlemagne, forever on the move, found them invaluable for himself and his men.

Trade was excellent; why not make it better? If people could be persuaded that shorter cloaks were more becoming, they might not notice that the price stayed the same while the cloth went further. Offa tried. Charlemagne's response was vigorous .... "Illa palliola" – miserable little cloaks; useless as bedding, worse in bad weather; most damning of all - when he dismounted "ad necessaria naturae tibiarum congelatione deficio!" – in short, his shinbones were frozen.

That friendship was patched up by a fresh consignment of the real thing, but Offa remained an opportunist. His friendship with the Pope seemed secure until the young King of East Anglia, Aethelbert, came under suspicion. His potential as a foe has not been defined, but Offa saw it as calling for drastic measures. He still had one unmarried daughter, and invited Aethelbert to Court as her bridegroom. The proposal was accepted with alacrity; it seems surprising that Offa failed to see in that a reason for reconsideration, but even though the young couple fell in love at first sight, the bridegroom was assassinated before he became a husband.

A storm erupted. Offa's daughter firmly refused any other marriage. "Murder" – the word met him everywhere, together with "treachery". The Pope heard the story as soon as fast horses could carry it. The only adequate expiation was to make the pilgrimage to Rome, leaving the realm a prey to enemies far more numerous and dangerous than Aethelbert. Alternatively, it would be wise to perform some spectacular penance.

So tithes, hitherto avoidable, became a grinding burden for a thousand years. A tenth of the stock; a tenth of the land produce; a tenth of earnings from such activities as milling, fishing, weaving, shearing; even the down from ducks and geese – all for Mother Church. Not just a single levy, once and for all, but to be paid annually; not just from Offa's property, but from every one of his subjects from the richest to the poorest – a compulsory exaction causing hardship and bitterness.

Like all human institutions it changed through the years. It began as compulsory by order of the King, and people got out of it whenever they could. However, the Church saw the possibilities; such a levy must not be lost. Within the next century and a half it was enforced by threat of excommunication. No longer a moral obligation in obedience to the liege lord, it became a stark alternative between the loss of a tenth of a man's whole property, however puny the gross total, and the eternal hell fire which was then vivid in every mind.

At first tithes were divided into four parts; one for the bishop, one for the clergy, one for church repairs, and one for the poor; by 1200 however, the wealth was so great that more complicated arrangements were needed. Firstly, tithes were divided according to kind:

1) arising from the soil; grain, fruit, wood, etc.
2) the produce of animals or poultry; calves, lamb, piglets, eggs, etc
3) indirectly from the soil; milling, fishing, spinning, etc.

Secondly, tithes were divided according to their value. The great or "rectorial" tithes were corn, beans, hay and wood. The little or "vicarial" tithes were the remaining items – animal products and those gained indirectly from the soil.

Since the Conquest, the parochial system had developed into a convenient network for the distribution of tithes. Parishes were small districts; each was a self-contained community with its own church and priest, himself often of peasant stock, and the lowest in the ecclesiastical hierarchy. The little, vicarial tithes were ear-marked for him, but they had to be stretched to the limit. Even if no superior claimed a share, the priest must still keep his house and the chancel in good repair. He must give hospitality wherever it was needed; vestments and service books must be well maintained.

Holders of rectorial parishes were better off, as they received the great tithes, but they had several smaller churches in their care, with assistant priests to be paid. Whatever their income, little tithes or great tithes, all parishes needed storage space. The need remained undiminished even after the dissolution of the monasteries by Henry VIII, for the monasteries' loss was immediately the gain of bishops or lay people who happened to be in favour at the time. Tithes must still be handed over – simply in a different direction. Neither was the Cromwellian war any help:

> As long as Oliver lived, the parson knew that he would still be able to venture into the fields of the retired corporal, and humbly carry off his lawful sheaves, at risk of nothing worse than ironical inquiries as to where he was at Worcester fight .... (Trevelyan)

Through the centuries many tithe payments were, by agreement, changed to cash transactions, but the burden was heavy, and continued until Parliament began to deal with it in 1836. Gradually, burdens were eased in both directions. The ill-paid lower clergy were no longer expected to maintain their chancels; by 1923 parochial church councils were largely responsible for such things. The depression of the 1930s brought further relaxation; at present "corn rent" is paid voluntarily by a small proportion of parishes, in much the same way in which parishioners contribute under the Planned Giving scheme. Barns which played their part in the old taxation still remain; many are still in use for various purposes, while others are preserved as beautiful examples of ancient architecture.

Barns Great and Small

Even within one county, there is great variety. Sizes vary, from the great cathedral-like barns such as Tisbury, which catered both for home produce and tithes, to those which, by comparison, are on the scale of a dolls' house. Built usually in the shadow of the parish church, they had only to accommodate the strange mixture of produce with which the incumbent was paid, together with the little he grew for himself. Structurally there are many points in common; these survivors of time and animosity were made of tough materials. Stone or brick walls; wood was better for grain storage, but too easy to burn. A thatched roof would have been better for the grain, but stone tiles were safer.

Thomas Davis, at the beginning of the nineteenth century, based his choice for Longleat barns upon centuries of inherited experience:

> .... as well calculated as possible for reception of corn, brick and stone being cautiously avoided, except for the foundations, and timber and weatherboard used in their stead, and the covering being usually thatch.

It was a counsel of perfection, but the medieval builders had to put security first.

Barns were usually rectangular, with two pairs of double doors facing each other; one pair in each long wall, and one pair taller than the other. A loaded wagon entered through the higher doorway, was unloaded, and departed through the opposite, lower doorway. Harvest time, particularly "catching weather", brought many wagons; a straight passage through, without turning, was essential. The doorways often had porches, in the side of which a small door admitted the monk or clerk whose duty it was to check the loads. Monastic establishments kept precise records.

Those paired doorways were very important at threshing time. With the doors wide open, there was a strong draught; grain was threshed on the ground between, and the chaff blew away. That part of the barn floor was usually wooden, to keep the grain dry; the greater floor area was beaten earth.

Ventilation was all-important. Whilst security meant stone walls and a tiled roof, the natural advantages of wood and thatch were lost, and must be replaced at least in part. Oillets were cut in the walls; slits in the stonework, sometimes just small holes, sometimes cruciform. They not only provided ventilation, but admitted owls and bats as a natural pest control.

The most striking feature of any barn was the internal roof structure. Between the top of the side and end walls and the high roof ridge, timbers supported the weight of the tiles with as much grace as those in churches. In each barn the timbering varied

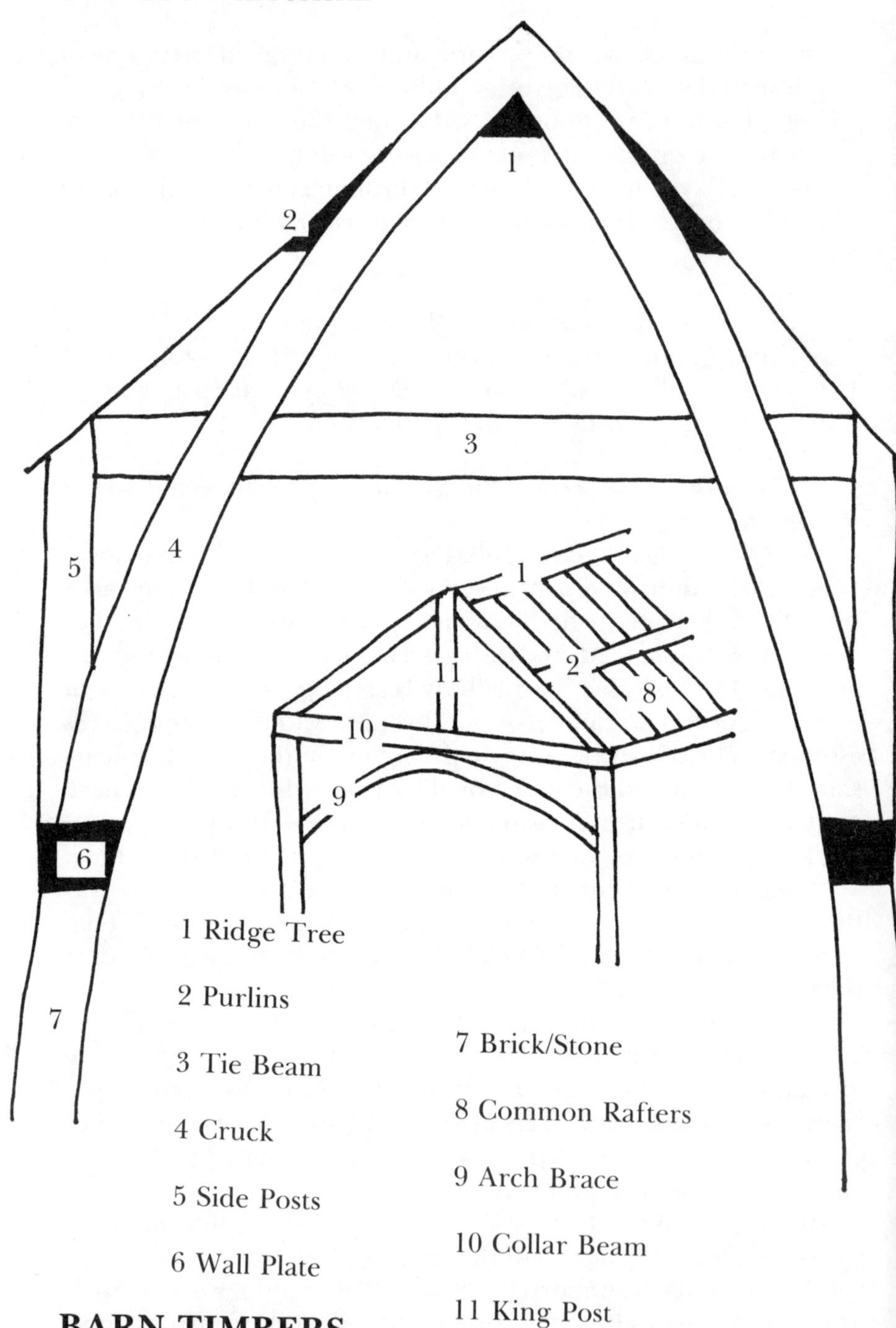

BARN TIMBERS

according to the size and shape of the building, and the material available. Where whole tree trunks were obtainable with the necessary curve, massive crucks rose from the wall plate to the ridge tree. Otherwise, smaller timbers were connected by joints which would do credit to modern craftsmen using modern tools. The effect was impressive, occasionally majestic; possibly ironic to folk weighed down by their burdensome tithes. Naturally there is a strong resemblance to church buildings – the roof timbers, the cruciform oillets, and in some cases cruciform barns; they were ecclesiastically built for ecclesiastical benefit. We have inherited their beauty without the burden.

Tisbury Barn, Place Farm

Also known as The Grange, as it was indeed one of the granges of Shaftesbury, granted to the Abbess in 984 by King Ethelred. Though within easy reach of the Abbey, an enormous barn was necessary to cope with the produce of the grange as well as local tithes; it is possible that tithes were not the main consideration here, during the Abbey's most prosperous times.

At first sight, security seems to have been a priority, for inner and outer gatehouses were built. The outer is thought to date from the thirteenth century, and has two entrances; one, high and wide enough to admit a loaded wagon, and the other, just the right size for a horse and rider.

However, the second gateway leads to the medieval farmhouse, while the great barn, 188 feet long and 32 feet wide, lies at right angles to the road, well past either gateway; a fairly easy target for the determined. Though not the longest barn in the country, it is one of the largest; built in the fifteenth century, most of the original fabric remains, but the old stone tiles on the roof have been replaced by thatch. There are three pairs of double doors, the central entrance having also a large porch. The three threshing floors give some idea of the size of the harvest centred upon this barn in addition to any tithes brought in. Small wonder that as late as 1830, when the new threshing machines were being introduced, there was a riot in the streets of Tisbury, with a battle between farm workers and the yeomanry brought in to quell them.

Inside the barn, the roof timbers are massive and beautiful, with upper and lower collar beams and great crucks rising from the wall

Tisbury Tithe Barn: general view

Tisbury Tithe Barn: gable end showing oillets, buttresses and thatched roof

plates. Thirteen bays have corresponding buttresses outside, and the end walls each have a central buttress with one each side. Perhaps the most beautiful feature of the building is the stonework; its warm creamy colour contrasts pleasingly with the immaculate surrounding lawns. Not an authentic view for purists, who might wish to see a working barn as it was during the Abbey's heyday; it has been dismissed as "neither so fine nor so interesting as Bradford," but the comparison is unfair. Tisbury has serenity and charm.

Bradford on Avon

Fine, and interesting. The comment referred to the great barn at Bradford; there is also a smaller, genuine tithe barn. Yet another little barn is marked on an official guide map as a tithe barn, but mistakenly.

The great barn, like Tisbury, was part of the Shaftesbury property, as was Barton Farm on which it stood, as well as numerous surrounding parishes. Bradford barn fulfilled the same function as Tisbury, accommodating crops from the grange, as well as tithes. It was built before Tisbury, in the fourteenth century; possibly by Gilbert of Middleton, Bradford's Lord of the Manor, and an avid collector of church offices. He was prebendary of five cathedrals; the salary due to him for each prebend came largely from tithes .... he was only ploughing the profits back into the business. However, so great a barn needed time to build; trees of the right size and shape for the crucks were not to be found overnight, and meanwhile there were crops to be gathered and more tithes to collect. They were put into a smaller, but useful building which stood at right angles to the site of the great barn. It had been there since the twelfth century; rather tall in proportion to its overall size, with a good stone-tiled, hipped roof: an excellent substitute. Present-day visitors tend to walk directly to the great barn, missing its predecessor which is, even now, sturdy enough to be useful.

The other small barn is in Newtown, just round the corner from Market Street. It has been beautifully restored, and is known as Priory Barn, but that name has only been in use since the middle of the last century, when the medieval house to which the barn belonged became the property of the Sisters of the Order of the

Holy Trinity. Since medieval times it had been a private residence known as The Methuens; built, not by a great landowner nor a wealthy ecclesiastic, but by a comfortable middle-class cloth manufacturer; a clothier.

The Sisters eventually departed, and the house, known by then as The Priory, reverted to private ownership until it was demolished in the 1930s. The little barn remains; a building offering much aesthetic pleasure, with no taint of past oppression.

The great barn also remains, offering similar pleasure in spite of its authentic association with tithes. Here and there in the outer walls a great block of sarsen glistens in the sunlight; other stone blocks bear the marks of the masons who cut them; not only for utilitarian identification, but a mark of pride in achievement. A considerable achievement indeed; those walls are two and a half feet thick along the sides, which, measured along the outside, are well over a hundred and seventy feet long. The end walls are four feet thick, rising to a height of thirty-nine feet at the ridge. Someone with a grievously enquiring mind has calculated that the stone tiles on the roof weigh approximately one hundred tons; easy to believe, looking at the many buttresses along the outer wall, needed to support so great a burden through the centuries.

It is even easier to believe, surveying the timbers which provide internal support for that roof. Curved crucks, supported by the wall plate, rise to various heights; some right up to the ridge tree, others as far as the collar brace; each one hewn from a single tree. Considerable repairs were necessary when the Ministry of Works acquired the barn some years ago; they were so expertly done that it is now difficult to tell which beams were jointed because enough trees of that length and curvature were unavailable even to Gilbert of Middleton; and which were originally as long as he could wish, but had to be repaired and partially replaced by the Ministry.

The north side has two large porches, each with a smaller side door; opposite, in the south wall, are two slightly lower exit porches. Between the western pair of doorways, the floor of beaten earth also has stone ridges, sufficiently far apart to allow cartwheels to pass along between them. It is as though somewhere in that barn there was a portable wooden floor, perhaps in sections, which could be laid down at threshing time and taken up afterwards. Those stone ridges are even, compared to the main floor of beaten earth;

Bradford on Avon Tithe Barn with its predecessor on the left: view from Barton Farm yard

Bradford on Avon Tithe Barn: interior view showing roof timbers and cross-shaped oillet

Bradford on Avon Tithe Barn: detail of the immense roof of stone

a floor made by the craftsmen who made the roof rafters and the great oak doors, would be sturdy and even. The eastern doorways have flat stones laid across the floor between them, on which a similar portable threshing floor might be accommodated. It has been suggested that the east end of the barn was completed some time after the rest; hence, perhaps, this different floor detail.

Nearby, across the Avon, there is still the fourteenth-century stone pack bridge, across which wagons used to bring the high-piled crops and tithes.

West Dean

This village is just inside the boundary between Wiltshire and Hampshire, and the barn is one of the busiest buildings on the farm to which it belongs. The brick walls were so well constructed that one looks twice, in disbelief, having heard various dates from eleventh to sixteenth century; however, the tiled roof, just a little crazy in places, adds persuasion. Officially it dates from the early fourteenth century, and was part of the estate of Mottisfont Priory, about ten miles away in Hampshire.

Mottisfont was never a wealthy foundation. It managed to scrape along until the Dissolution, when the Priory buildings were converted into a country mansion, and the barn, with the farm on which it stood, became manorial property. Yet nothing has diminished the atmosphere of that old barn. A few modern windows have been put into the south wall for the sake of the cows now using it as a byre, but the original small oillets remain in the opposite wall.

The entrance is on the north side; there is no porch, but the high double doors face a lower pair opposite. There are thirteen bays, and the overall length is 170 feet, with many outer buttresses. The heavy roof timbers are white with age, and it is easy to imagine the deer coming in from the New Forest as they did in times past; this was also a deer barn. In hard winters room was found – tithes or no tithes – and here they found shelter and food. As Edith Olivier wrote, Waleran himself might have built that barn; Waleran, the Norman ranger of the New Forest, responsible for the care of deer and trees.

It was a flight of fancy, but standing in that quiet yet still functional barn, the fancy once again took wing.

Melksham

After three great barns, this is in the dolls' house class. It stands almost in the shadow of St Michael's church, which is of Norman origin. Melksham barn is prim, neat and rectangular, except for a nineteenth century attachment at one side. The parish was well-endowed and desirable. In 1200, when King John discovered that the See of Salisbury was poverty-stricken by his standards, he thought of a remedy:

> We have found the Commune (common fund of the Chapter) of Sarum to be trifling and meane, we have granted and dedicated the Church of Melksham with the chapel of Stolus. (Erlestoke) .....

Melksham included the neighbouring parishes of Seend and Shaw, and was a valuable acquisition. In the fifteenth century, the barn was built; though the Great Tithes went elsewhere, the Vicarial Tithes, unusually lavish, remained with the incumbent. The income was good, but out of that the Vicar had to pay the

Melksham Tithe Barn: a school since 1877 and now converted into flats

priests of Seend and Erlestoke. His barn was just about the right size.

At the dawn of the nineteenth century, education was an increasingly important issue, and the Church was one of the leaders in its promotion. By 1840, St Michael's National School was built, between the church and the barn. It was for older children; the infants were taught in a couple of rented rooms in a nearby cottage.

The little complex developed; in 1850, a teacher's house was built; two years later, the school was enlarged. By 1877 the tithe barn came into service, adapted as a school for the boys. After yet another enlargement, both boys and girls used the school building, while infants were promoted to the tithe barn.

Now, the schoolhouse and the tithe barn stand at either side of the old playground, which is adorned with flower beds. Both buildings have been beautifully converted into flats without losing any of their original character. The school still has its old-fashioned tiny belfry, and the tithe barn could never be mistaken for anything else, with its three-stage buttresses and the long oillets in the steep gables. A picturesque corner, tucked away in workaday Melksham.

Biddestone

Here is a place (John Aubrey would have said) of enchantment. Near-perfection, as villages go, and they go very well in Wiltshire. When you have hardened yourself to turn your back upon the village, move southward for a hundred yards or so. There, behind a precision of topiary, is a manor house fit for a princess; it was built in the seventeenth century, long after Queen Matilda, the Iron Lady of the twelfth century, had granted the tithes of the parish to the Priory of Monkton Farleigh. Though not a small house, it is not too big to look cosy, and its symmetry is aesthetically satisfying without being stiff. From the side, it is approached through a formal garden. At the front, two buildings stand at right angles to it, one on each side.

The right-hand building is a small barn; stone and tile, with a stair up the side to a doorway under the eaves, a little like the smaller barn at Bradford on Avon, but without the hipped roof. Facing that from the opposite side is another barn which is younger; the date on the gable is 1706. It may well have been a necessary addition if the farmlands around had increased their output. If the Lord of the Manor of that time was receiving tithes - and presumably the Farleigh monks were not - he probably needed the extra storage space.

Since then, tithes have dwindled away. One Biddestone tithe barn seems to be of use as a stable and tack room, but its younger companion has had an elegant transformation. The long oillet is still there in the end gable, high up towards the roof tree, but below, there is a high, wide window. Extra windows have been cut along the side wall, and a low central gable has been added - all meticulously in keeping with the overall personality of the barn. A little bridge passage connects it to the house. It is a barn-ballroom; beautifully achieved, and fit for a princess; the princess who, with her prince, lives there in Biddestone Manor .... There was something else that Aubrey said: "This searching after Antiquities is a wearisome task." Not always.

Lacock

Ela, Countess of Salisbury, was a great lady of the thirteenth century. Her family owned estates in Normandy; an ancestor had fought alongside the Conqueror at Hastings. Her husband was William Langespée, son of Henry II and his best-loved mistress, Rosamund; half-brother of King John, and his closest friend even though John usually lost when they gambled; a man of charm and wealth, renowned as a soldier.

Ela also had charm, though possibly her wealth had something to do with the proposals she had to repulse even before she became a widow. It was wealth in the millionaire class, but she used it for religious purposes. Charities, benefactions, foundations; Wiltshire owes its most beautiful building to her. Salisbury cathedral is only one of the churches which she founded, but that is where Langespée lies.

She also built an abbey, at Lacock. On the edge of the village there was a meadow site with woodland and a clear river; one of the manors which were part of the Salisbury family property; hers, together with various services to be performed by the tenants. The abbey was therefore one of the most wealthy, owned and endowed

Lacock Tithe Barn: interior view showing roof timbers

Lacock Tithe Barn: interior view showing splayed oillets

by Ela; since she was also its Abbess, many aristocratic girls took the veil there, and their large dowries increased the wealth still further. Tithes, as usual, came in promptly. A tithe barn was needed, but Ela was fully occupied by the Abbey and its affairs. A barn already stood alongside the old road leading to the Abbey; long, straight, and with plenty of space - it was about ninety feet in length, with large doors. The stone tiled roof was supported by great crucks, curved braces and collar beams. Had it held tithes for Lacock's Norman church of St.Cyriac? As had Bradford's smaller barn, perhaps, for the Norman church of Holy Trinity?

Tithes came in on carts and pack mules; some on the donors' backs. Many came across the pack bridge or the ford, at By Brook. The original bridge was destroyed by floods, but the modern replica is good, with the low parapets typical of pack bridges. The animals – horses or mules – carried bulky packs which hung low on either side; had the parapets been of normal height the packs would have broken open or fallen off in bumping against the stone. Imagine such an accident to tithes; the need to return home for a second load from the already depleted store ....

The great tithe barn was completed in the fourteenth century. It is an odd shape; rectangular, except that the southern end curves to follow the shape of the road as it bends towards the Abbey. It has the usual pair of double doors at the roadside, but the highest pair at the entrance porch is reached only by following the road alongside and behind the long barn. This brings one face to face with the entrance, not only to the tithe barn, but to the long barn, which has double doors higher and wider than those opening to the road, but exactly corresponding in position. A ramp would be necessary to bring carts over the high step; but one would also be necessary in the tithe barn, in returning carts to the street.

The intriguing point is that the fronts of both barns are, so to speak, at the back; away from the street as it has been for many centuries. In those early days, were tithes brought by a shorter route? – from the pack bridge, across the old market place in front of the church, and along the footpath still marked on the National Trust map; or was the explanation even simpler? Just that at harvest time, when so many carts and pack animals arrived, there was more space for them on the other side than the narrow street could provide.

In spite of its irregular shape, the tithe barn is not ungainly. Seen from the porch side, it has ecclesiastical dignity; the timbers of those great doors, wide oak planks, are like the rafters of West Dean barn - white with age. The porch has had much wear and repair through the centuries; there have been two different inspection doors at various times. In the body of the building, the stone walls measure four and a half feet to the wall plate, after which great crucks take over almost as impressively as at Bradford, with some elegantly curved braces – also, as at Bradford. The same workmen as at Bradford? – it seems likely.

Here and There

Stratton St Margaret kept its barn, near the church, until about two years ago. Then came a sensitive architect, commissioned to build a small residential complex on the site.

An old farmhouse melts into its new surroundings as though it had never known anything else; the new dwellings have a rustic aura. Where did the old barn end, and where did they begin?

In 1445, it was said that "the grange within the King's Manor at Margrete Stratton was roofless and the thatch rotten." Yet it remained for many centuries. With that modern artistry before me, I felt that its sturdy grace had not yet departed.

In Stockton, the dream of Thomas Davis comes true: "Three barns at least, with three threshing floors, to avoid mixing the different kinds of grain .... built on low stone pillars to keep out rats and mice .... the covering being usually thatch." There they stand, immaculately thatched - "three barns at least" – a group of buildings almost too neat to have much to do with practical farming, clustered around the soft lawns and flower beds of the manor house. So beautiful a picture, I was lost in delight, and forgot to sketch, or even to take notes. Whether the thatch of those memorable barns covers brick, stone or timber walls I have no idea; only that the delight will return whenever I hear the name of that village.

At Hill Deverill, the barn is very large. It has three porches, many buttresses, dates from the fifteenth century, and is cast in the same mould as the tithe barns at Tisbury and Bradford on Avon, but from the start it has been the property of private families. At first, the Hulle family; then, for three hundred years, the Ludlows; then

Hill Deverill Barn: interior view of the roof

Hill Deverill Barn: exterior view showing the three porches

the Cokers. It would be easy to dismiss it from one's list of tithe barns, having no ecclesiastical connections. Yet it might be so. At the Dissolution, the Ludlow family were in possession; they were not among the great hangers-on at Court; not among those who kept in with Master Thomas Cromwell in case there were any jewelled garments going a-begging after their owners had been executed. But at home in Wiltshire, monastic houses were perishing in all directions. Edington, Amesbury, Shaftesbury, Kington St.Michael, Lacock, Wilton, Malmesbury, Salisbury (St.Nicholas Hospital, an invaluable little Augustinian foundation), Monkton Farleigh, and even little Ivychurch and Axford - the pickings were rich. Strange, if an important local family failed to acquire at least some advantage, such as the right to collect a few of the tithes which hitherto had gone in another direction; in which case that enormous barn bacame a tithe barn, in a quiet way.

A small point which has nothing to do with tithes, but everything to do with hardship and oppression. I mentioned that in 1830, the streets of Tisbury were the scene of a battle between the yeomanry and farm workers protesting against the new threshing machines which were going to put them out of work. In the 1830s that was a terrible, ever-present threat.

Towards the end of that century, Elyard, in his book on a selection of old Wiltshire houses, wrote that Hill Deverill Barn was said to be haunted. Not by the shade of any unquiet human, but by a machine, which could be heard rattling in the barn. That machine which folk had longed to see destroyed, and of course it never was; instead, a legend grew about an unquiet, ghostly machine which presumably had come to an untimely end. Folk memory wreaked a strange, oblique vengeance.

Cherhill

From a barn with a ghost to a barn which became one. At least, it was reported as still standing and dwarfing the neighbouring church; but that was twenty years after having been demolished. Until 1956, Cherhill was the last wooden barn in the county, and one of the largest. It had survived since the fifteenth century, but caused much concern during its last hundred years. The priest of Cherhill Parish from 1860 to 1891 was William Charles Plenderleath, the historian, and he left a clear description of the barn, which was rectangular, measuring 111 feet in length:

> There are four stone porches, two each side, like transepts. The interior consists of seven bays, and is divided into a nave and aisles by a row of large posts standing upon masonry bases, and running up to the purlins of the roof. Across these come the collar beams, and above again, small collar beams, with king posts between the two. Supporting the lower collars are strong curved braces, and above them and against the king posts straight struts, but in the two central trusses these are united into one large curved brace, coming right down to the level of the wall-plates. The walls were all originally of narrow panel work raised upon a stone plinth about three feet high ....

The weight of the roof was becoming too much, even for those elaborate timbers. The whole building developed a list to the west, and in 1938 the owner asked the Office of Works to estimate the cost of repair. The answer, four thousand pounds, would have purchased at least eight family houses. Neither the owner nor any interested society could pay that price, and strong rumours arose: the barn was going to be dismantled and exported to the United States.

Some temporary work was done, and timber was stored there during the 1939 war, but delapidation grew steadily worse. In 1956, with any further repairs estimated at over twelve thousand pounds, the barn was demolished.

In 1976, an author wrote that the great barn at Cherhill dwarfed the parish church standing next to it. Quite a ghost ....

Bradenstoke

Bradenstoke was a priory with a pedigree. It was founded in 1142 by Walter d'Evreaux, the devout Norman whose grand-daughter, Lady Ela, founded Lacock Abbey. His wealth, like hers, would seem to have been boundless; he decided, he ordered, he endowed. High on a steep hillside, the buildings grew: undercroft, dorter, chapel, guest house, prior's lodge, refectory, and tithe barn. Augustinian monks came from the Norman monastery of Saint-

The remains of Bradenstoke Priory, bereft of its Tithe Barn since 1937

Wandrille, and went devoutly into action. The order was noted for its hospitals, and Bradenstoke started one at Wootton Bassett, about four miles distant. After a few years some of the monks set out for Lancashire, where they built Cartmel Priory, but after four centuries, the Dissolution struck them all; bloodshed at Cartmel, but only buildings at Bradenstoke. In the second half of the seventeenth century, Aubrey noted that Broad Hinton House,

Bromham House, and Cadnam House were built of "the ruines of Bradstock Abbey." The first two were burned down in the civil wars, and "Cadnam is propt for fear of falling." He was no romantic, but by 1833 a correspondent of the *Gentlemen's Magazine* had acquired the fashionable taste for ruins:

> The windows, buttresses and lofty parapet, with one square turret on the north, appear through almost the whole extent of the vale of the Avon beneath .... parts of Somerset, Gloucester and Berkshire intersected by the winding Avon with long green pastures lie beneath as in a map .... on the right, as in a foreground, is another hilly eminence dark with oak, almost under our feet. The ancient arches of the principal building, now partly dilapidated and used as a farmhouse, are entire ....

It passed from owner to owner. Paul Methuen of Corsham sold it in 1863. By 1879 visiting antiquaries saw that undercroft and refectory had been divided into smaller rooms for the use of farm workers. No one made much of that. The awakening began slowly when in April, 1928, *Country Life* published the usual announcements of properties for sale:

> Especially appealing to Archaeologists and lovers of Medieval Architecture. Bradenstoke Abbey near Chippenham Wiltshire. Under 90 miles of London ....
> This wonderful fragment of an ecclesiastical establishment .... rich in architectural features of unusual interest.
> *Stands boldly on a hill commanding a glorious panorama over four counties.*
> Easily capable of enlargement, it contains six bedrooms, bath, three or four reception rooms including the Abbot's parlour where there is the original chimneypiece dated 1350; there is also a wonderful crypt with massive stone undercrofting; electric light, septic tank drainage; splendid water.
> *Garage, stabling, and magnificent Tithe Barn*
> 40 acres in all. Very moderate price

The Priory had been sold so many times; no one noticed that there were no takers. For a year, everything was suspiciously quiet. No more advertisements, no buyer named. May 1929 brought a bombshell. Wiltshire Archaeological Society received a report that Bradenstoke Priory Barn was being demolished; presumably by the purchaser, but the workmen, when questioned, declared they had not been told their employer's name. Worse; a tarpaulin had been erected to conceal the depredations.

Strange, that a newspaper tycoon from the United States should imagine that his little secret could be hidden behind a tarpaulin. William Randolph Hearst, multi-millionaire with a passion for ancient buildings, was dismantling the Priory and the tithe barn. Each piece was carefully numbered as it was taken down, ready for re-erection at St.Donat's castle, his home in Glamorgan.

No one believed that. Photographs of the buildings, before Hearst and after Hearst, were published in *Country Life*. Before, it was a ruin, but attractive. After, stones lay in fragmented masses – there seemed to be precious little numbering there. Letters swamped the newspapers complaining of such vandalism. One editor thought fit to publish a reminder:

> It should be mentioned that Mr Hearst bought Bradenstoke in order to reconstruct it as an addition to St.Donat's Castle, his residence in Glamorganshire. However regrettable the destruction, and however perplexing to future antiquarians the addition of a priory to a medieval castle, it must be borne in mind that Bradenstoke was for long in the market without any organised attempt being made to purchase it for the nation or otherwise to preserve it.

The protests were thunderous. Questions were asked in the House, and the Prime Minister was asked to interfere. Ramsay Macdonald replied that the affair had gone too far; he could only legislate against future events. In any case, the Priory and the barn were not going to the U.S.A. – only to Glamorgan.

By this time, the only remnants on the site were the undercroft and the north turret. The Society for the Protection of Ancient Buildings bought the before-and-after photographs; underground stations in London were full of posters: "Protect Your Ancient Buildings. Bradenstoke, Wiltshire, before and during demolition for the sake of old materials."

Hearst threatened legal proceedings; the Society obliterated the words "for the sake of old materials" and the posters remained. There were even allegations that he ran an anti-British press; but he was silent; he had run out of steam. A previous owner of the Priory wrote in his support, to the *Wiltshire Gazette*. If people felt so strongly, why had no one started a subscription? The Priory cost more than it was worth in repairs; the last owner could not find the necessary £500, so why should Mr Hearst be expected to spend that on a building situated where it was no use to him?

The editor replied that no one had been told what was intended until the destruction was all but accomplished. This stung Mr Hearst into reply. The owner had wanted to sell. The priory had been on the market a full year with no offers:

> Sir Charles Allon (architect) informed me that a proposal had been made .... by an American firm to buy the building and transport certain parts of it to America. Sir Charles advised that we buy it and preserve it at St.Donat's. I agreed to this. The building was carefully demolished and stored, and will be re-erected at St.Donat's unless the Government or the Society for the Preservation of Ancient Buildings desires to acquire it and erect it somewhere else ....

Everyone else had run out of steam too. However, it is not difficult to recognise the source of the 1938 rumours about Cherhill barn.

There was one final comment from Sir Charles: "He (Mr Hearst) had bought the building and the barn .... taken them with great care to St.Donat's .... has decided that it shall be rebuilt in its original form and thus saved for the nation as a work of art ...." From 1931 to 1937, barn and priory were therefore in store at St Donat's Castle, if the statements of Mr Hearst and his architect were reliable. No building took place there; Bradenstoke was gaunt and empty; the depression and the Abdication redirected the nation's attention.

Then, out of all the confusion, came general delight at the approaching coronation of a loved and reliable monarch. Mr Hearst's true stature appeared; in spite of all the abuse he had received, he generously put it aside and joined in the celebration

Lacock Tithe Barn: exterior view with tourists showing obliquely angled gable end

just as though he were an Englishman. On the second of April 1937, a press announcement appeared. The Bradenstoke tithe barn was to be made into a large reception room at St Donat's Castle. It would be finished in time for the Coronation, which Mr Hearst intended to celebrate in style.

More in sorrow than in anger, his architect, Sir Charles, replied in the very next issue. Not the barn .... the priory was to be used for the large reception hall .... If anyone knew, surely the architect was that person? Bradenstoke Hall was duly built at St.Donat's, and impressed the glittering array of guests.

At present it has an even busier existence. St.Donat's Castle has become Atlantic College, where young people of many nations live and study together. The priory of William d'Evreaux is, in a modern way, fulfilling its founder's intention; Bradenstoke Hall is in constant use, for the good of mankind.

But in view of the statements of William Randolph Hearst and his architect, one wonders whether a careful search through the castle might possibly unearth one tithe barn in sections; numbered and packed and awaiting assembly. Rather like those toys supplied in kit form; but this time, bring your own glue.

Bibliography

Water Meadows

G.Boswell *A Treatise on Watering Meadows* (London 1801)

Thomas Davis *Wilts. Agriculture* 1794

Rowland Vaughan *His Booke* ed E.B.Wood (London 1897)

Wiltshire Archaeological Magazine, Vol.17, Jackson; Vol.55, p.115, Kerridge, vol.58, Attwood

A.G.Street *Round the Year of the Farm* (O.U.P. 1935)

John Aubrey *Natural History of Wiltshire*

Economic Historical Review, Kerridge

Hatcher Review Vol.2, No.14: Cowan

Bettey *Rural Life in Wessex 1500-1900*, p.26

Victoria County History, Kerridge: *Water Meadows*

Wilts Record Office 1473/18

White Horses

Notes and Queries 1896, p.478

Plenderleath *White Horses of the West of England*

Herodotus V11, 55

Guide to Ancient Monuments (H.M.S.O. 1936)

Blackford *Manor and Village of Cherhill*

Marples *White Horses and Other Hill Figures*

Revd. Francis Wise *Observations on the White Horse and other Berkshire Antiquities*, 1742

Sir Richard Colt Hoare *Ancient History of Wiltshire*, 1812

Dom Illtyd Trethowan *Downside Review*, July 1939

Revd. W.P.Gresswell *The Story of the Battle of Edington* (Wessex Press 1910)

Camden's Britannica (ed. Gough) 1806, Vol.1, p.146

Wiltshire Archaeological Magazine, Vols. 4, p.306; 52, p.396; 59, p.183; 77 (Bastian 1982)

Sarsen Stones

Wiltshire Archaeological Magazine, Vols. 6, 31, 52, 63

Aubrey *Natural History of Wiltshire*

Richard Symonds *Diary of the Marches of the Royal Army during the Great Civil War* (1859 ed. Charles Edward Long, Camden Soc.)

Gentlemen's Magazine, 1796 p.466; 1816 lxxxvi pt.2

Notes and Queries, 2nd. series V11, p.141

Stukely Brentnall *W.A.M.* 1946

Brentnall, H.C., *W.A.M.* 1946

Grigson *Shell Country Alphabet*

Christopher Chippindale *Stonehenge* (Thames and Hudson 1984)

Atkinson, R.J.C. *Prehistoric Temples of Stonehenge and Avebury, Stonehenge and Neighbouring Monuments* (H.M.S.O.)

Patrick Crampton *Stonehenge of the Kings* (Baker 1967)

Dew Ponds
Wilfred Blunt *Aspects of England* (Richards 1937)
The Spectator Nov.16th, 1901: Article
Wiltshire Archaeological Magazine Vol.XL, p.444
Antiquity, Vol IX, p.347
Gilbert White *Selborne*
Edward A.Martin *Dew Ponds; History, Observation and Experiment* (Laurie, 1914)
Wiltshire Folklife Vol.3, no.2, 1980-1 *The Cruse Family of Imber* by Rodney Cruse
Alfred Pugsley *Dew Ponds in Fable and Fact* (Country Life, 1938)
Thomas Davis *Wiltshire Agriculture* op.cit.
Brentnall and Carter *The Marlborough Country* (O.U.P. 1932)
H.W.Timperley *Ridge Way Country* (Dent 1935)

Blind Houses
Wiltshire Archaelogical Magazine, vols. 25, 46, 47
Notes and Queries, vols. 1, 4, 5
Gentlemen's Magazine: vols. 8, 9
Victoria County History, vol. 7
Wiltshire Record Society, vol. XXXVII
Mr Hunt (J.P.) notebook
Papers of the relevant parishes: Wiltshire Record Office
John Howard: *State of the Prisons*, 2nd. ed.
Sidney and Beatrice Webb: English Poor Law History, part 1
English Prisons under Local Government

Tithe Barns
Thomas Davis *A General View of the Agriculture of the County of Wiltshire*, 1794
Colin Platt *The Abbeys and Priories of Medieval England* (Secker and Warburg 1984)
Bryan Little *The Abbeys and Priories of England and Wales* (Batsford 1979)
Hugh Braun *English Abbeys* (Faber 1971)
Frank Bottomley *The Abbey Explorer's Guide* (Kaye and Ward 1981)
Edith Olivier *Wiltshire* (Hale)
Pevsner *Wiltshire* (Penguin)
Hutton *Highways and Byways of Wiltshire* (Macmillan)
Blackford *The Manor and Village of Cherhill*
Wiltshire Archaelogical Magazine Vols. 24, 34, 35, 37, 44, 63
The Archives of Wiltshire Archaelogical Society (Devizes Museum)
Francis Bath *Dorset and Wessex Barns, 1980*